Eating
Disorders

P9-CKR-495

Eating Disorders

New Directions in Treatment and Recovery

Second Edition

BARBARA P. KINOY, EDITOR

COLUMBIA UNIVERSITY PRESS NEW YORK

Columbia University Press
Publishers Since 1893
New York   Chichester, West Sussex

Copyright © 2001 Columbia University Press
All rights reserved

Library of Congress Cataloging-in-Publication Data
Eating disorders : new directions in treatment and recovery /
Barbara P. Kinoy, editor.—2nd ed.
p. ; cm.
Includes bibliographical references and index.
ISBN 0–231–11852–X (cloth : alk. paper)
ISBN 0–231–11853–8 (pbk. : alk. paper)
1. Eating disorders. I. Kinoy, Barbara P.
[DNLM: 1. Eating Disorders—therapy.
2. Eating Disorders—psychology. WM 175
E14812 2000]
RC552.E18 E2853 2000
616.85'26—dc21   00–055497

∞

Casebound editions of Columbia University Press books
are printed on permanent and durable acid-free paper.

Printed in the United States of America
Designed by Audrey Smith

c 10 9 8 7 6 5 4 3 2 1
p 10 9 8 7 6 5 4 3 2 1

Figure 2.1 from Dr. Martin Katahn, *Beyond Diet:
The 28-Day Metabolic Breakdown Plan,*
W. W. Norton, 1984. Used by permission.

Figures 2.2, 2.3, and 2.4 from
Eating Disorders: Nutrition Therapy in the Recovery Process. 1990.
Dan W. Reiff, MPH, RD.
Aspen Publishers, Inc., 1992. Used by permission.

*To our patients' children and grandchildren, and to our own . . .
the future generations, that they may be less encumbered than
their forebears by mind, body, and food dissonance in their growing up, and that they may enjoy food, love, and self-esteem in just
the right proportions . . . the golden mean.*

CONTENTS

FOREWORD

Disturbances in human eating behavior are hardly new phenomena. Uncontrollable hunger and binge eating were described by ancient Greek and Roman physicians long before the birth of Christ, and the syndrome of anorexia nervosa was clearly recognized and named more than a century ago. Literally for hundreds of years, clinicians have been struggling to assist individuals unable to control their food intake.

Unfortunately, there is much we do not understand. We do not know, in any meaningful sense, the fundamental causes of eating disorders. Our best understanding is that these disorders are multifactorial in origin—that individuals are at risk because of a combination of as yet incompletely identified biological, psychological, and social characteristics. And just as there does not appear to be a single cause, so, too, there does not seem to be a single, universally effective treatment.

Although serious deficiencies mar our understanding of these problems and our ability to treat them, real progress has been made. Some signs of that progress are reflected in the fourth edition of the American Psychiatric Association's *Diagnostic and Statistical Manual (DSM-IV)*, which was published after the first edition of this book. *DSM-IV* not only includes revised criteria for anorexia nervosa and bulimia nervosa but also provides tentative criteria for recognizing binge eating disorder. This disorder, characterized by recurrent binge eating without the regular use of inappropriate compensatory behavior required for the diagnosis of bulimia nervosa, is a common behavior among obese individuals. The promulgation of these criteria has already spurred new research into the characteristics of such individuals and the development of treatment interventions.

Notably, in *DSM-IV*, eating disorders are no longer grouped with disorders usually first diagnosed in childhood or adolescence. Instead, for the first time, eating disorders constitute a separate section of their own. This change from previous editions of the *DSM* reflects the fact that many individuals with eating disorders do not present for treatment until adulthood. It is also a response to the growing importance to health care providers of recognizing and treating these disorders.

This book meets another need. It is a highly accessible, readable, and useful collection of the wisdom of knowledgeable clinicians who have practiced at the Wilkins Center for Eating Disorders. Many other volumes on eating disorders are theoretical treatises or detailed explorations of treatment strategies, often removed from the difficult realities of patient care at the end of the twentieth century. Such works are very valuable but leave a gap which this volume helps to fill.

The authors of each of the essays address critical "real world" issues; they provide guidance for assessing and treating individuals with eating disorders and for assisting their families. The descriptions of what clinicians actually do are both informative and refreshing, and the reports of successes resulting from skilled and collaborative treatment are impressive. Equally impressive are the vivid depictions of the enthusiasm and optimism of the staff at the Wilkins

Center. Their attitudes inform all the chapters and are a strong source of hope for both practitioners who endeavor to treat eating disorders and patients who struggle with them.

B. Timothy Walsh, M.D.
William and Joy Ruane Professor of Psychiatry
College of Physicians and Surgeons
Columbia University
Director, Eating Disorders Research Unit
New York State Psychiatric Institute

PREFACE

In 1994, in the first edition of this book, I wrote that "only a few years ago anorexia nervosa and its related illness, bulimia, were conditions not ordinarily seen in the course of one's professional life." Since then, it is likely that most professionals in the health, psychology, and education fields have encountered someone suffering from an eating disorder and have learned to recognize the variations and combinations that may be presented. These conditions have not gone away; more are recognized, more are treated, and there are many prevention programs in colleges and high schools that did not exist in the early nineties. Hence our offering of this updated edition. And it's unlikely that these conditions will abate soon. Statistics vary, but the 1 percent statistic for young women suffering from anorexia nervosa in industrialized societies remains fairly constant, with the percentage of those suffering from bulimia ten times higher

(Barber 1998). Special groups of the population, namely, college-age women, suffer markedly. Jennifer Biely, director of the Eating Disorders Awareness and Prevention organization (EDAP), recently estimated that 5–7 percent of America's twelve million undergraduates are afflicted. (PEOPLE, 1999)

In most countries where the disorders are identified, it is estimated that 90 percent of those suffering from an eating disorder are female. The concentration in the teenage and young adult years makes it a disturbing impediment to health. An alarming number of prepubescent girls in the United States are already worried about weight and are beginning to diet. It is evident that the syndrome finds its way into cultures of plenty, or seeming plenty, where starvation is not the common rule. One may safely generalize that atypical eating and its consequences are rooted in our society, reflecting—often painfully and grotesquely—our miniworlds of strivings for identity, value, self-esteem, and ease from distress.

Various causes have been identified in different centuries. In medieval times, spiritual and mystical religious connections were seen; more recently, connections have been made to the family environment, the individual's attitude, and medical considerations. In the early part of the twentieth century, medicine increasingly focused on possible pituitary defects or other physical abnormalities. A swing toward psychoanalytical considerations from the 1940s on brought deeper understanding of the vulnerabilities in personality development that made disruption and distortion of eating possible. Most recently, the expansion of theory and new findings have given us much knowledge and many tools that can be applied to treatment approaches. Among these are behavioral theory and technique, self-psychology, emphasis on maturational stages, relational aspects of living, nutritional information and protocols, and psychopharmacological innovations. Careful theorists and thoughtful pioneer practitioners have paved the way, among them Professor Arthur H. Crisp in England (*Anorexia Nervosa: Let Me Be*, 1980) and, in the United States, the late Dr. Hilde Bruch (*The Golden Cage: The Enigma of Anorexia Nervosa*, 1978).

In addition, the burgeoning feminist movement has encouraged a more specific exploration and understanding of the development of the girl-child into womanhood, thus pointing up the societal and psychological hazards to healthy growth. We are more aware of the strain on the young girl's identity formation as she views disparate images in the media and advertising. For instance, is she to mirror the sexy, slim, and sometimes sullen siren or the seductive childlike Lolita? What will make her seem the same as others so that she feels she "belongs," or what will make her appear "different" so that she feels unique and appealing? Is intellectuality to be pursued, or will such a pathway discourage popularity? Expressions of unease take different forms for different groups of people. Girls and women have often focused on appearance—if the body is perfect, then all will be well. Years ago, when Karen Horney called for a new view of the female psyche, she commented on the way a group of women she had studied reduced their failures in relationships with men to seeming ugliness or a real or fancied defect in the body. She added that one of her patients had "fasted for weeks when her brother told her that her arms were too fat" (Quinn 1987). And now, more than six decades later, we still see unhappiness reflected in body dissatisfaction, often with a distorted body image. In many of the following chapters the reader will find the conflict and contradictions of our times echoed in the patients' efforts to reach cognitive and emotional equilibrium.

A consolidation in the findings of sociological, psychological, and physiological studies show many factors that promote the development of eating disorders. Along with the physical state, we now consider matters of dependence, independence, sexuality, identity, gender, self-image, body image, obsessionalism, addiction, fear, depression, anxiety, and a host of other qualities that are ingredients of human existence. A *multidetermined* etiology is thought to be a more valid picture of causation. A treatment approach combining many different modalities, each addressing some aspect of the illness, is generally recognized as a thorough and effective plan for bringing about recovery.

The following collection of papers provides hands-on accounts of how professionals in this field approach their work by combining theory and knowledge in their own idiosyncratic way, from the vantage point of their particular discipline. The idea for this book was generated largely from the Wilkins Center for Eating Disorders, where the director, Diane W. Mickley, M.D., has ensured a rich and intensive learning experience for those practitioners who have joined in a team effort to study and treat those who applied for care. The reader will find that the authors, for the most part, have used female pronouns—*she, her*—in their writings. This usage reflects the predominance of females over males who are known to suffer from eating disorders. While much discussed here is applicable to males, our views rest on our greater clinical experience with the female patient population. Boys and men have vastly different cultural and physiological imperatives that are the infrastructure in their development, and these have to be considered in their treatment.

Some of the authors have elected to write about aspects of their work that particularly engage them. Others have chosen to give an overview of their role (Thode on family therapy, for example, or Kahm on nutrition). Increasingly cognitive-behavioral therapy has become regarded as a potentially effective tool, which is reviewed in the Wegners' chapter. Roloff's chapter describes a current project utilizing some of the tenets of cognitive-behavioral therapy. A treatment dynamic, managed care, will be discussed in these and other chapters, as well as in the Ortmeyer chapter, describing a more lengthy treatment required to address the psychodynamic and developmental issues involved. The fact of managed care will be discussed in a separate chapter by Ortmeyer, describing both its enabling factors and its restrictive qualities related to treatment. Some authors discuss the therapist's own reflections and countertransferential experience as they relate to personal angst and perplexities in the past, and often in the present, aroused and recalled through the work. Cases are described in different stages and levels of progress. The clinical beauty of a collaborative team is in the initial determination, the ongoing evaluation as to the appropriate treatment modality, the "fit" of therapist and patient, and the effectiveness of the whole.

Our implicit theme is *recovery*, for all therapeutic endeavors include that goal. The term, however, may mean simply that the symptoms are alleviated or that the person has developed other modes of living that are more productive, satisfying, and interrelated with others. In-between variations on being "better" also exist, depending on one's individual makeup and position in life. Whether partial, complete, or relative, recovery does occur; *something* brings it about. Our authors contribute their views on some of the factors that facilitate recovery. By no means has there been an attempt to cover all possible aspects, given the intangible complexities of human interaction. The therapist's clinical observations, the patient's assessment, and other people's responses combine in the consideration of recovery.

Despite several follow-up studies revealing much significant material, hard data about what actually ensures recovery remain elusive. It has recently been said that "almost nothing is known about what facilitates recovery on an experiential level" (Hsu et al. 1992). In this same article it was reported that in a follow-up study twenty years later, six recovered anorexic patients considered the following as being important factors in recovery: *personality strength, self-confidence, being ready, and being understood.* And in reviewing research, Johnson and Connors (1987) observed, "This issue of patient character structure and the resulting ability and/or motivation to comply with anxiety-provoking demands of a particular treatment program is probably a very important variable, and one that remains relatively unexplored." Since then, research has continued to seek out those factors that bring about improvement.

The contributors to this book have had extensive dialogue with recovered people. In our afterword, the reader will find patient reports compiled in a study by the Wilkins Center in 1987 and a summary of other research currently in progress at the time of this writing. Recovered patients often join us to participate actively in support groups, hot lines, and community presentations. Some have entered the medical or psychological professions themselves, thus utilizing what they have integrated into their own everyday lives.

We have therefore considered what "works" from the viewpoint of the clinician and of former patients who have talked of their experience in illness and in treatment. These papers, in discussing the workaday world of the practitioner, continue an essential dialogue. The very real burden of "how to" is a constant source of reflection for the practitioner whose expertise is continually challenged by life's infinite variation.

Barbara P. Kinoy

References

Barber, Nigel. 1998. "The Slender Ideal and Eating Disorders: An Interdisciplinary 'telescope' model." *The International Journal of Eating Disorders* 23, no. 3 (April): 296.

Hsu, L. K. George, Arthur H. Crisp, and John S. Callender. 1992. "Recovery in Anorexia Nervosa: The Patient's Perspective." *The International Journal of Eating Disorders* 2, no. 4 (May): 341.

Johnson, Craig, and Mary E. Connors. 1987. *The Etiology and Treatment of Bulimia Nervosa*, pp. 302, 303. New York: Basic Books.

People Weekly. 1999. "Out of Control," 52–72; quote, 54. April 12.

Quinn, Susan. 1987. *A Mind of Her Own: The Life of Karen Horney*, 265–66. New York. Addison-Wesley.

ACKNOWLEDGMENTS

We wish to acknowledge our indebtedness to colleagues throughout the country and beyond, in many different professional disciplines brought to bear on the problem of eating disorders, who labor in research, theory, and practice. In addition, many of us have participated in organizations such as the American Anorexia/Bulimia Association (AA/BA) made up of practitioners in the field and people who have felt the effects of these disorders, either in a family member or in themselves. Such involvement has afforded us a broad range of learning beyond the consulting room, in various aspects of education, self-help efficacy, advocacy, and prevention efforts. We therefore express our appreciation for this avenue of growth.

To our other colleagues at the Wilkins Center for Eating Disorders we owe much appreciation. Although they have not written about their work in this volume, they continually contribute to the field in various ways. We have mutually shared and expanded our learning, sometimes with humor, sometimes with earnest argument, and always with camaraderie and many long phone conversations!

Those who staff the Wilkins office and keep all systems working are to be thanked as well. They are responsible for the welcoming atmosphere that prevails at the Center. Toni Hall, MSW, CSW, served as the coordinator in the original formation of the book, often providing the link between the writers and editor when distance required it. We thank her for her help in the initial planning stages.

We thank the innumerable patients' families who have put their faith and hope in our abilities. That they could do so, and that they could be supportive of our efforts even during many difficult phases of treatment, is an important part of the whole process.

Most of all, we thank those patients who have shared so generously, who have taught us so much, and who have entrusted us with participation in their journey toward recovery.

Proceeds from this book will go to the Alison D. Warren Memorial Fund, a nonprofit organization furthering accessibility of treatment and education to numbers of young people.

Alison Warren (1962–1989) died of anorexia and bulimia. Through the memorial fund, created in her memory, her family and friends have perpetuated her spirit of caring for others. Administered by Greenwich High School in Greenwich, Connecticut, in collaboration with the Wilkins Center for Eating Disorders, the fund provides staff training, education for students and parents, and primarily treatment scholarships to promote early intervention and care for students with eating disorders.

CONTRIBUTORS

Debra Bader, CSW, BCD: Former therapist, Wilkins Center for Eating Disorders; private practice.

Sarita Broden, CSW: Individual and group therapist, Wilkins Center for Eating Disorders; private practice.

Margaret Goldkopf-Woodtke, LCSW: Former individual and group therapist, Wilkins Center for Eating Disorders; private practice.

David Greenfeld, M.D.: Clinical professor of psychiatry, Yale University School of Medicine; director of Psychiatry, Wilkins Center for Eating Disorders.

Annika Kahm, BS: Chief nutritionist, Wilkins Center for Eating Disorders, Greenwich, Connecticut; member, Academy of Eating Disorders.

Nancy King, LCSW: Clinical director, individual and group therapist, supervisor, Wilkins Center for Eating Disorders; private practice; Board of Directors, Academy for Eating Disorders; former board member, American Anorexia/Bulimia Association.

Diane W. Mickley, MD, FACP: Founder and director of the Wilkins Center for Eating Disorders, Greenwich, Connecticut; past president, American Anorexia/Bulimia Association, New York; founding member and board member, American Academy for Eating Disorders; research associate, Department of Psychiatry, Yale University School of Medicine.

Inge Ortmeyer, LCSW: Director of staff, Wilkins Center for Eating Disorders; supervisor; social worker, Norwalk High School, Norwalk, Connecticut; private practice.

Phyllis Roloff, R.N.: Director of Nursing, Wilkins Center for Eating Disorders.

Suzan J. Ryan, Ph.D.: Former staff member, Wilkins Center for Eating Disorders; private practice.

Nancy Thode, MSW, LCSW: Family therapist, Wilkins Center for Eating Disorders; private practice.

Andrea Z. Wegner, Ph.D.: Psychologist, Wilkins Center for Eating Disorders, private practice.

James T. Wegner, Ph.D.: Psychologist, Wilkins Center for Eating Disorders, private practice.

Editor: *Barbara P. Kinoy, CSW, Ph.D.*

Formerly, director of professional development, staff therapist, and supervisor, Wilkins Center for Eating Disorders.

Editor/author, *When Will We Laugh Again: Living and Dealing with Anorexia Nervosa and Bulimia*. New York: Columbia University Press, 1984.

Former columnist, "In My View," *American Anorexia/Bulimia Association Newsletter*, New York.

Contributing author, with Adele M. Holman, DSW, and Raymond Lemburg, Ph.D., "The Eating Disorders: An Introduction," in *Eating Disorders—A Reference Source Book*, ed. Raymond Lemburg, with Leigh Cohn, Revised edition. Phoenix, Ariz.: Oryx Press, 1999.

Senior consultant, Wilkins Center for Eating Disorders.

Member, Academy of Eating Disorders

Eating
Disorders

Introduction

DIANE W. MICKLEY

I am often asked why the Wilkins Center was established. In 1981 I had a general medical practice in Greenwich, Connecticut. As one of the few female physicians in town, I saw many women, especially young women. Several appeared with anorexia nervosa.

The approach to eating disorders in those days was simple. Because anorexia was a psychiatric problem, the patient was referred to a psychotherapist. I found, however, that many therapists were reluctant to treat anorexics. A psychiatrist whose work I respected told me candidly that he did not find he could help such women. Others accepted patients for years of treatment, but the patients remained as ill as before.

I saw an anorexic teenager whom I referred after much difficulty to a child psychiatrist. When her sister became anorexic later that year, the best we could do was to find a therapist many towns away. Her parents commented that the two therapists gave conflicting advice. The parents felt uninvolved and at a loss as to how to help their daughters. They observed that while the girls discussed their feelings in treatment, they remained unable to eat and continued to lose weight. One sister required a long-term psychiatric hospitalization and was discharged still unable to maintain a normal weight. This kind of experience contributed to the belief that eating disorders simply were not treatable.

The idea of a treatment center began to take shape. Perhaps we could bring to our community the techniques producing the best results elsewhere. I began to visit some of the early specialists in treating eating disorders: in New York, in Baltimore, in California, in Boston, in Canada. There was no consensus among them about what approach to use, but many had suggestions and generously shared their experience and support.

When the Wilkins Center for Eating Disorders opened in November 1982, we had a nucleus of professionals committed to improving care for patients with eating disorders. In the ensuing years, the Center has been involved in the care of more than three thousand anorexic and bulimic patients. The staff expanded quickly to almost thirty, allowing each member to provide the intensive care many patients required. We used offices throughout Westchester County, New York, and Fairfield County, Connecticut, so that patients might have frequent visits with less travel. While most continue to come from Connecticut and New York, we also treat patients from other states as well as from Europe, Latin America, and Asia, who elect to reside in the area temporarily to receive state-of-the-art treatment.

The professionals involved in the Wilkins Center developed an extraordinary level of commitment, cohesiveness, and expertise. Seminars, study groups, and supervision, as well as extensive clinical experience, promoted individual and collective development. The staff's personal and professional closeness facilitated a team approach: Individual and family therapists, group leaders, physicians, nurses, and dietitians collaborated to provide coordinated and comprehensive care. High patient volume enabled us to target subsets with specialized needs: younger teens, high school and college students, single adults, married women, pregnant patients, and eating disordered mothers. Services also expanded to encompass the needs of patients whose eating difficulties coexisted with other psychiatric problems, including substance abuse, personality disorders, or the effects of trauma.

The primary focus of the Wilkins Center has always been clinical treatment but that has expanded to include research and prevention. Affiliations were formed primarily with colleagues at Yale University, but also with those at Harvard University and Columbia University. Wilkins staff served as founders and leaders of national advocacy groups, government task forces, and professional organizations. The staff donated time to public education, at local schools, through media interviews and in television appearances.

Although the Wilkins Center initially targeted anorexic and bulimic patients who were typically close to normal weight or underweight, we were approached by an increasing number of patients who were overweight. Some seemed to have a biological problem—a genetic tendency to be heavy—compounded by an American lifestyle high in calories and low in exercise. Others, however, especially "compulsive overeaters," shared many features of our bulimic patients. They were preoccupied with the pursuit of thinness, often with endless cycles of dieting and then bingeing. Depression (and sometimes alcoholism) was common in such patients and their families.

A new category of eating disorder was proposed in 1992: binge eating disorder (Spitzer et al. 1993). These men and women binge but they do *not* purge. They tend to fail traditional weight-loss programs but seem to benefit from treatments similar to those developed for bulimia (McCann and Agras 1990). People who fulfill the criteria for the "binge eating disorder" represent up to 2 percent of the general population, from 30 percent to 50 percent of patients in hospital weight-loss programs, and up to 70 percent of people in Overeaters Anonymous. Thus treatment developed in the past decade for bulimia may benefit a far larger population than originally envisioned.

With skilled specialists and expanding treatment options, the majority of patients with eating disorders can hope to get better. Treatment for eating disorders is not magical. It takes sophisticated care, hard work, and time, often far longer than we wish. Unfortunately the current revolution in health care may significantly restrict access to experts and limit both intensity and length of treatment. Yet with sufficient care, large numbers of patients can and do recover. Many resolve adolescent issues, develop heightened self-esteem, improve relationships, and expand coping skills in ways that provide lifelong benefits.

This book is an effort to share some of what we have learned from our patients and one another, as well as some of the advances in the field of eating disorders during a pioneering era.

Eating disorders are complex syndromes occurring in diverse people and settings. They vary in the physical toll they take. Some patients are physically stable, others are in acute medical danger or developing chronic health problems. Some are fairly well nourished, others restrict or binge to the exclusion of any normal eating.

Psychological well-being also varies widely. Eating disorders may be precipitated by the developmental needs of adolescence or by an acute crisis. They may compound long-term difficulties with low self-esteem, obsessionalism, or depression. They may coexist with anxiety, panic attacks, or personality disorders. They may worsen in seeming paradox despite recovery from alcoholism, acceptance at college, or a wonderful social relationship.

Patients come with different attitudes toward treatment. Some may feel they have no problem or can recover "on their own"; others have had so much treatment that they have lost hope. One person may long to resolve basic difficulties in psychotherapy, while another, convinced that the problems are biological, may seek medication. Some wish to come alone; some prefer to be with parents or spouse; some seek the sharing and support of a group.

Families, too, vary in their understanding of eating disorders, past experience with treatment, and perceptions of what is best for their daughter. They may seek a suitable inpatient program or hope that intensive outpatient care will avert the need for hospitalization. Parents may have to juggle the demands of a child's illness with the needs of their own marriage, their careers, aging grandparents, and other offspring. Emotional and financial resources and burdens differ from family to family.

To complicate this picture further, professionals, too, may vary in their approaches or may offer conflicting advice. If parents suspect an eating disorder, where can they go for evaluation? If a person seeks treatment, what kind and what setting is best? If a patient is in therapy or on medication but continues to struggle, would a change jeopardize progress or speed recovery?

Over the past two decades we have been confronted by these issues every day. We have the luxury of comprehensive services: medical, nutritional, psychiatric, psychological, individual therapists of many styles, family and marital therapists, and a wide array of groups. All the professionals on the staff have extensive clinical experience and many years of specialization in eating disorders. Many have particular strengths: working with adolescents, with parents, with alcoholics, with victims of abuse, and so on.

Having worked together on hundreds of patients, we are used to collaborating. We can trust the physician to monitor medical problems. We expect the dietitians to be doing cognitive and behavioral work on the reality of eating. Therapists will be working to help patients understand what needs their symptoms are serving. Groups can lessen isolation. Staff professionals work in conjunction with one another, sharing observations, problems, and goals. Our answering machines fill with long messages as we share significant developments from a patient's session. Though we work exclusively on an outpatient basis, we are able to provide the intensity of treatment, as well as the sense of being in a therapeutic community, that facilitates progress in hospital settings.

Each patient needs a treatment plan suitable to her needs. Would outpatient or hospital care be preferable? Should patients work individually or in family therapy? Will nutritional counseling be useful? Should medication be avoided or encouraged? When might group therapy be helpful? Not only must we decide what to recommend but we must enlist and maintain the patient's involvement and the parents' trust (if the patient is a child or adolescent) if treatment is to proceed and succeed.

Sound recommendations require a thorough evaluation. This includes a careful history, psychological assessment, review of physical findings, and laboratory tests. A plan is developed in conjunction with the patient and, if appropriate, with the patient's family. Four to six weeks may be required for patient, therapist, and nutritionist to begin to work together enough to assess potential success. Throughout treatment, however, periodic review is necessary to adjust care, as needed, to a person's current situation.

Eating disorders impact health and emotional well-being. They also complicate major and minor life decisions. Should she go to camp? Should she go to (or back to) boarding school or college? Is it wise to travel or study abroad? To ski, run, or play varsity sports? How should families handle food shopping and mealtimes? How do they respond to "I feel so fat"? Members of the treatment team collaborate with patients and families in working out the many immediate issues that continue throughout the extended time it may take to resolve eating disorder symptoms and then to ferret out their psychological underpinnings.

The following papers describe the approach of some of the Wilkins Center staff. They offer a variety of perspectives. But which is best suited to each patient and at what point in treatment? There is no cookbook recipe for treating eating disorders. The success of treatment hinges on its suitability for the person involved and its adaptation to her evolving needs over time. This requires the skills of experienced specialists in a good working alliance with the patient and the patient's family.

References

McCann, U. D., and W. S. Agras. 1990. "Successful Treatment of Non-purging Bulimia Nervosa with Desipramine." *American Journal of Psychiatry* 147:1509–13.

Spitzer, R. L., S. Yanovski, T. Wadden, R. Wing, M. D. Marcus, A. Stunkard, M. Devlin, J. Mitchell, D. Hasin, and R. L. Horn. 1993. "Binge Eating Disorder: Its Further Validation in a Multisite Study." *International Journal of Eating Disorders* 13, no. 2: 137–53.

1

Medical Aspects of
Anorexia and Bulimia

DIANE W. MICKLEY

Eating disorders involve a complex interplay of physical and emotional factors. The medical complications of anorexia and bulimia can be life-threatening but may give no outward warning symptoms. Attention to health realities must accompany (or even precede) therapy to provide the time and safety for recovery.

ANOREXIA

Most patients with anorexia do not see themselves as starved, since they do eat and often very healthy foods such as salads. But just as a car with the best tires and oil cannot run without gas, no amount of "healthy" foods can make up for inadequate calories. Without sufficient calories, the body slows its metabolism, compromises vital functions like circulation, and destroys muscle to provide the fuel that isn't coming from food.

The military published a famous study decades ago simulating prisoner-of-war camps by subjecting healthy men to starvation (Keys et al. 1950). Their behavior soon showed many "anorexic" features: They obsessed about food constantly, ate meals slowly and used strange rituals, and felt depressed and tired; once allowed to resume normal eating, they binged for months afterward. Some anorexic symptoms, then, may be understood as a biological defense against starvation. Preoccupation with food, fatigue, and sometimes depression can be tolls of malnutrition alone, which improve when weight is regained.

Patients with anorexia are often plagued by constant thoughts of food and weight. They may experience depression, fatigue, and sleep disturbance, as well as feeling cold, getting bloated or constipated, or growing fine body hair (called *lanugo*). Many anorexics, however, insist they feel fine, or they minimize their discomforts and continue to work hard, get good grades in school, perform athletically, or exercise compulsively. This makes it hard for patients, family, friends, even doctors, to realize the dangers of their condition.

Not only do anorexic patients perform in a vigorous fashion that may mask the severity of their illness, but the tolls of starvation may not show on a simple physical examination. Electrocardiograms may not show the kind of heart weakening that occurs, and blood tests are often normal or seem only mildly amiss. Because of this, anorexics often insist that they are healthy rather than in jeopardy; others may also be similarly mistaken.

WHEN IS LOW WEIGHT UNHEALTHY

Being underweight takes a major toll on the body. But what is underweight? Anorexics often feel that if other women they know or magazine models can be very thin, then they should be able to be that thin as well. Unfortunately, what seems fair is not always what is healthy. Some lucky individuals maintain a marvelously low cholesterol despite high-fat diets, while others have dangerously high cholesterols even though their diets are ideal. Similarly, people come in many genetically determined body types. A few people have bodies that can tolerate being extremely thin; the vast majority do not.

People inherit many different body types. Efforts to drive weight below biologically predetermined levels result in all sorts of physical and emotional tolls, including loss of menstrual cycles and an intrusive preoccupation with food. In addition, those who exercise frequently or are active athletes increase their percent of muscle mass. Since muscle weighs more, athletes may require weights that are higher than their inactive peers.

A simple formula exists that roughly estimates the *ideal weight* for a young woman of average bone size, although many women should weigh more than this formula predicts. Take 100 pounds and add 4 pounds for every inch over 5 feet in height (108 pounds for 5 feet, 2 inches; 116 pounds for 5 feet, 4 inches; 124 pounds for 5 feet, 6 inches; and so on). For a more solid build, adjust by adding 5 pounds for every inch over 5 feet (110 pounds for 5 feet 2 inches; 120 pounds for 5 feet 4 inches; and so on). For a very slight bone size, adjust down to add only 3 pounds for every inch over 5 feet (106 pounds for 5 feet, 2 inches; 112 pounds for 5 feet, 4 inches; and so on). Few factors allow for ideal weights lower than these, although a variety of factors (exercise, body type, older ages) result in ideal weights that are higher than these.

The term *critical weight* defines the minimum weight the body needs for healthy function. Critical weight is about 90 percent of ideal weight. Within 10 percent of ideal weight, as estimated above, some people can be thin but healthy. Below 90 percent of ideal weight, significant physical compromise occurs, even when its tolls are not readily apparent. Thus an average-sized female who is 5 feet, 5 inches, might have an ideal weight of 120 pounds. Her critical weight would then be 10 percent less (that is, 120 pounds minus 12 pounds) or 108 pounds. Critical weight may not be enough for a woman to menstruate or participate in competitive sports, but it gives us a rough guideline of a minimum for adequate health. Below critical weight, major physiological impairment occurs, regardless of how well a person feels.

Two other factors can obscure the impact of dietary restriction. First, youngsters not finished with puberty may not *lose* weight; they may just get taller without gaining the weight to go along with it.

These pre-teens will fail to gain weight and will ultimately stop growing, but they may become anorexic without actual weight loss. Second, girls who are overweight to begin with may lose dangerous amounts of weight and have some of the physical tolls of anorexia but may not seem as dramatically underweight because of the extra pounds they began with.

PHYSICAL TOLLS OF ANOREXIA

As noted earlier, anorexic patients don't think of themselves as starved, because they do eat some food. Their bodies, however, show the profound effects of starvation. Loss of menstrual periods is one of the most obvious signs of anorexia. Even more dangerous, however, are the invisible tolls of anorexia, especially on the heart, brain, and bones. In a single patient, tests may not demonstrate the severity of physical compromise. However, research studies document the unseen damage.

The impact of anorexia on the reproductive system is reflected in the interruption of menstrual function. Girls who become anorexic in the pre-teen or early teenage years may fail to begin menstruating despite other signs of puberty. They may also miss crucial stages of breast development. Older anorexics stop having menstrual periods unless they happen to be on birth control pills. Interestingly, periods may stop before weight loss occurs for up to one-third of anorexics. Menstruation resumes with adequate weight restoration, but recent data suggest a higher miscarriage rate in women who have had anorexia. Anorexics who are not fully recovered also have a greater incidence of infertility. If fertility treatments are used to induce pregnancy at marginal maternal weights, there is an increased frequency of infants with low birth weights (Abraham, Mira, and Llewellyn-Jones 1990).

Anorexia is associated with a fulminant form of osteoporosis. Lifelong bone strength depends on the accumulation of bone mass during adolescence. With anorexia, bone formation is impaired and bone breakdown is accelerated. This leads to bone thinning, which may be seen within six months of menstrual cessation or with the delayed onset of menstruation in premenarchal girls. It is also seen in young men with anorexia. The osteoporosis of anorexia is typically most severe in the lumbar spine. This can lead to painful fractures, preclude impact exercise (such as jogging), and lead to vertebral compression fractures, which create a stooped posture. Unfortunately, even women who recover fully from anorexia may be left with irreversible osteoporosis. Although low estrogen levels may contribute to the bone loss of anorexia, hormone replacement therapy has not been demonstrated to be of protective value. Nor do the medications that benefit postmenopausal osteoporosis appear to help. The only remedy of proven effectiveness at this time is rapid restoration of weight until menstrual function resumes (Grinspoon, Herzog, and Klibanski 1997).

The tolls of anorexia on the heart are especially dangerous. The body burns muscle to provide fuel as starvation progresses. Heart muscles, like those in the arms and legs, become smaller and weaker. Blood pressure falls, heart rate slows, and the mitral valve may prolapse. To protect vital core organs, the heart reduces circulation to the periphery, visible as *acrocyanosis*, the bluish-purplish discoloration of the fingers and toes seen in many anorexics, especially in the cold. Cardiac impairment also limits the ability of the heart to increase oxygen delivery to the tissues in response to exercise. Because of this, continued exercise in underweight patients is especially dangerous. Even at rest, however, low weight anorexics are at risk of irregular heart rhythms that can lead to sudden death (Cooke and Chambers 1995).

Anorexia also causes loss of brain tissue, documented by x-ray studies using both Computer-Aided Tomography (CAT scans) and Magnetic Resonance Imaging (MRIs). Cognitive testing shows associated impairment in thought processes. These changes may be subtle, especially initially. With recovery, brain mass appears to improve, at least partially (Swayze et al. 1996).

Stomach function is impaired by anorexia. There is a stomach emptying delay, so food may "sit there," as it often feels to patients (Kamal et al. 1991). Liquids are more readily digested than solids, and frequent small portions are better tolerated than large meals. Stomach function corrects after months of improved intake, but medication to promote stomach emptying may be useful temporarily if symptoms are severe.

The malnutrition of anorexia has other pervasive effects on health. Bone marrow function may be impaired, interrupting the formation of any line of blood cells. The result is anemia (low counts of red cells that carry oxygen), leukopenia (low counts of white cells that fight infection) and/or thrombocytopenia (low counts of platelets that are needed to stop bleeding). The immune system may be compromised. Levels of thyroid hormone (thyroxine) may fall, cholesterol may rise paradoxically, and liver function may be amiss. Though some patients feel deceptively well, others experience fatigue, coldness, insomnia, constipation, and many other distressing symptoms

Every underweight anorexic is in some degree of danger. Regaining weight is urgent. It is the critical prerequisite both for physical safety and for emotional recovery. Weight restoration may be possible working intensively with an outpatient treatment team that includes not only a psychotherapist but also a physician and dietician experienced in the recovery process for anorexics.

Hospitalization may be necessary if weight is very low (less than 25 percent of ideal body weight), if medical complications arise, or if outpatient weight gain is not immediate (within weeks) and sustained. Inpatient eating disorder programs have been developed at certain psychiatric hospitals. They must be experienced at normalizing weight during hospitalization while developing the skills to maintain weight following discharge. The closer the patient is to ideal weight at the time of hospital discharge, the less likely relapse will occur requiring further hospital admissions. Recent changes in health care have greatly reduced the coverage of full hospital treatment for anorexia. Day programs are now used increasingly, hoping to avert or shorten residential hospital care.

Weight gain is a very difficult process. Patients continue to fear being fat. Minimal increases in calories or volume seem excessive. Exercise often must be stopped temporarily. Psychotherapy and nutritional counseling may provide support and education to foster progress toward a healthy weight. As weight is regained, work in psychotherapy may help patients and families understand and modify stressors that contributed to the illness. However, weight restoration is the initial priority and is essential to preserve health and build a foundation for psychological recovery.

BULIMIA

Anorexia and bulimia sometimes overlap. About 50 percent of patients with anorexia develop bulimic symptoms during their illness. This subset of patients has an especially high incidence of both medical and psychiatric difficulties. The vast majority of patients with bulimia are of normal weight. In fact, up to one-third were overweight in the past.

Bulimics binge; that is, they have episodes of uncontrollable eating, usually consuming large volumes of food. For some, however, binges are subjective; a normal meal or a forbidden food is experienced as excessive. Fearing weight gain, bulimics compensate for their binges. *Nonpurging bulimics* engage in excessive dieting or exercise. *Purging bulimics* most commonly induce vomiting. Laxatives, diet pills, or diuretics may also be used in futile attempts to lose weight

Though some patients with bulimia feel well, most experience both emotional and physical discomforts. Bulimics often feel ashamed, secretive, isolated, depressed, out of control. Like anorexics, they are often preoccupied with food and weight in a constant, bothersome way that soon intrudes on other spheres of their lives. Patients with bulimia may also suffer from a wide range of distressing symptoms, including wide weight swings, insomnia, weakness, heartburn, bloating, swollen glands, and irregular periods.

PHYSICAL TOLLS OF BULIMIA

Bulimia can cause pervasive physical damage. Often, however, this is mainly internal and may not produce visible signs. As with anorexia, the physical examination and laboratory tests may be deceptively normal (Becker et al. 1999).

The purging of bulimia usually impacts the gastrointestinal system. Chronic vomiting bathes the esophagus in stomach acid, causing inflammation. Esophageal tears are also common, resulting in pain and the vomiting of blood. The sphincter between the esophagus and stomach becomes impaired, and reflux is common. The stomach empties poorly, producing bloating after meals.

Vomiting depletes the body of potassium and other electrolytes. This danger is compounded by low weight, as well as abuse of diuretics and laxatives. While many bulimics have normal blood tests, electrolytes must be monitored to be safe (Greenfeld et al. 1995). Low potassium may cause muscle weakness, but it can be asymptomatic and still lead to respiratory arrest or irregular heart rhythms, causing sudden death.

Dental problems are rampant in bulimia. Enamel on the lingual surface of the teeth becomes eroded. Cavities and gum disease are common, and patients may lose all their teeth at an early age. Salivary glands in the cheeks (parotids) and lymph nodes under the chin (submandibular) are often enlarged. This can produce swelling and a "chipmunk cheek" appearance, which usually improves once bulimia resolves.

Most patients who abuse laxatives choose the cathartic type. These drugs work *for* the bowel, causing it to be unable to function on its own after a while. In addition, laxative abuse causes metabolic changes that can lead to painful kidney stones. Very high doses of laxatives that contain phenolphthalein have also been reported to cause pancreatitis and encephalitis. Ironically, using laxatives to lose weight is misguided, since *laxatives do not remove calories.* Calories are already absorbed before food reaches the part of the colon where laxatives work. Laxatives may cause temporary weight loss by taking out water, but this dehydration leads to rebound fluid retention. Bulimics who abuse laxatives may experience edema each time they try to stop. Special treatment regimens can facilitate laxative discontinuation without the severe water retention that plagues some patients.

Most deadly among the forms of purging is the abuse of Ipecac, a syrup used to induce vomiting in children who are poisoned (Greenfeld et al. 1993). Many patients try it once and find it so unpleasant that they avoid further use. However, the emetine in this product has a long half-life, leaving the system extremely slowly. This means that repeated use, even two or three times a week, can cause high levels to accumulate in the body. Since emetine is itself a muscle poison, ongoing use may produce myopathy with arm and leg weakness or sudden heart failure.

Bulimia may cause both gynecological and obstetrical problems.

Irregular or even absent menstrual periods occur in many women with bulimia, even those of adequate weight. Some studies show increased fetal risks to women afflicted with eating disorders during pregnancy. Such patients clearly require special care.

Up to 20 percent of women with bulimia have problems with alcohol or drug abuse. Often patients are already in recovery by the time they come for eating disorder treatment. Obviously, however, those with active substance abuse as well as bulimia have a whole additional set of medical risks. Inhospital treatment can be especially useful in this situation.

Both anorexia and bulimia have specific physical dangers. Both require careful medical monitoring. Some patients will feel quite ill, others deceptively well. All should have a physical examination, blood tests, usually an electrocardiogram, and other studies as appropriate. Although one hopes that this exam and all the tests will be normal, we know that this *in no way* shows the patient to be free of medical danger. Medical treatment is geared to averting some of these risks, lessening symptoms, and promoting recovery.

References

Abraham, S., M. Mira, and D. Llewellyn-Jones. 1990. "Should Ovulation Be Induced in Women Recovering from an Eating Disorder or Who Are Compulsive Exercisers?" *Fertility and Sterility* 53, no. 3: 566–68.

Becker, A. E., S. K. Grinspoon, A. Klibanski, and D. B. Herzog. 1999. "Eating Disorders." *New England Journal of Medicine* 340, no. 14: 1092–98.

Cooke, R. A., and J. B. Chambers. 1995. "Anorexia Nervosa and the Heart." *British Journal of Hospital Medicine* 54:313–17.

Grinspoon, S., D. B. Herzog, and A. Klibanski. 1997. "Mechanisms and Treatment Options for Bone Loss in Anorexia Nervosa." *Psychopharmacology Bulletin* 33, no. 3: 399–404.

Greenfeld, D., D. W. Mickley, D. Quinlan, and P. Roloff. 1993. "Ipecac Abuse in a Sample of Eating Disordered Outpatients." *International Journal of Eating Disorders* 13, no. 4: 411–14.

Greenfeld, D., D. Mickley, D. M. Quinlan, and P. Roloff. 1995. "Hypokalemia in Outpatients with Eating Disorders." *American Journal of Psychiatry* 152:60–63.

Kamal, N., T. Chami, A. Andersen, F. A. Rosell, M. Schuster, and W. E.

Whitehead. 1991. "Delayed Gastrointestinal Transit Times in Anorexia Nervosa and Bulimia Nervosa." *Gastroenterology* 101:1320–24.

Keys, A., J. Brozek, A. Henschel, O. Mickelsen, and H. L. Taylor. 1950. *The Biology of Human Starvation.* Vol. 1. Minneapolis: University of Minnesota Press.

Mickley, D. W. 1988. "Eating Disorders." *Hospital Practice* 23, no. 11A: 58–79.

Swayze, V.W., A. Andersen, S. Arndt, R. Rajarethinam, F. Fleming, Y. Sato, and N. C. Andreasen. 1996. "Reversibility of Brain Tissue Loss in Anorexia Nervosa Assessed with a Computerized Talairach 3-D Proportional Grid." *Psychological Medicine* 2, no. 2: 381–90.

Recovery Through Nutritional Counseling

ANNIKA KAHM

The nutritionist opened my eyes to a new world—how to eat normally.   —Outcome Study by the Wilkins Center, 1987

Is there really a need to educate eating disordered patients about nutritional balance and healthy eating habits? Don't they know this already? Haven't they read books about dieting, and haven't they been counseled about the importance of good eating habits by physicians and therapists? Frequently, they do know. However, in my experience their nutritional knowledge is mostly related to how they can diet to lose weight in order to feel better about themselves and to give them a sense of control. An educational approach emphasizing the value of nutritional counseling may therefore be helpful to resistant patients when their denial of nutritional needs impedes recovery. However, good nutritional knowledge may not automatically lead to healthy eating behavior.

Nutrition, the physical nurturance of the body and mind, is a reflection of personal growth. How one nourishes oneself with food mirrors how one feels and cares about oneself. Taking risks with food paves the way for taking parallel risks in our lives.

But in today's society many have a goal to be thin. We certainly are given enough messages telling us that "thin is in" and "if you are thin you will be happy, marry the right upper-class man, get a better job, and be able to fit into the clothes the models advertise on television and in magazines." Being thin today means being thinner than ever. Twenty-five years ago Miss America would be roughly 5 feet, 10 inches, and weigh about 140 pounds. Today our models at that height have lost 25 pounds and weigh a mere 115 pounds—if not less. Although we would all like to be slender we must realize that less than 2 percent of the population is naturally "model thin"; the rest of us have to like ourselves because of who we are—not because of how thin we are.

To gain control over our weight, we need to be able to listen to the body's signals of hunger and satiety (being full). It is important to realize that not all of us eat only when we are physically hungry; few of us stop when the body tells us it has had enough. For someone suffering from anorexia, bulimia, or a binge-eating disorder, hunger can either be denied, tuned out, or will often be experienced as a bad feeling—a feeling of being out of control. Some of the anorexics with whom I have worked are incapable of tuning in to the hunger and instead learn to live with it, getting used to being hungry all the time. Because they may feel out of control regarding certain issues in their lives (for example, parents' separation, loss of a boyfriend, and so forth), starvation often becomes part of their control. It feels safe for them because they will remain thin and will thus be accepted. But because her body never received the food it tried to get by sending hunger signals that she denied, the anorexic will have to live with a constant food obsession. I have been told by many that, as long as they keep denying their hunger by restriction, food obsession is their enemy, following them day and night. Some bulimics, on the other hand, will eat continuously to avoid this scary sensation and then are likely to purge when they feel too full. This makes sense since their ultimate fear is to gain weight. Reaching satiety may mean to them that they have had too much, especially since their goal usually is to lose weight.

THE TREATMENT TEAM

In the middle of this century, eating disorders like anorexia nervosa and bulimia nervosa were treated mainly with psychotherapy (Bayer et al. 1983). Because our knowledge, understanding, and awareness of these disorders have increased in the last two decades, the demand for improved treatment naturally follows.

In some cases of severe anorexia where the body weight has dropped because of starvation and the patient is malnourished or dehydrated to the point where she is unable to function, immediate help is required to prevent death. Today this help should consist of a multimodal treatment program involving medical consultation, pharmacotherapy, individual therapy, group therapy, family and marital therapy, and nutritional counseling (Johnson and Connors 1982). In some instances, hospitalization is essential as part of the program.

The symptoms of the severely bulimic patient are usually less threatening but can include the risk of cardiac arrest resulting from electrolyte imbalances, dehydration, and, frequently, ipecac syrup abuse (Andersen 1988). Overdoses of laxatives or abnormally low potassium levels have frequently caused the bulimic patient to end up in the hospital emergency room. In addition to the anorexic patient's treatment team (physician, psychiatrist, therapist, and dietitian), a dentist is often consulted to treat enamel erosion in the bulimic patient caused by acidity during self-induced vomiting (Reiff and Reiff 1992). A detailed description of symptoms appears in the first paper in this book, in Diane Mickley's description of the illnesses that comprise eating disorders.

Because an eating disorder generally is the symptom of underlying emotional problems, these problems have to be acknowledged and resolved in order for the patient to recover. The psychotherapist is crucial in helping the patient, but that does not mean that the chaotic eating behavior will magically disappear when emotional problems are resolved. A dietitian who has an understanding of the psychodynamics of eating disorders is the most qualified person to address issues related to food- and weight-related behavioral change (Reiff and Reiff 1992).

Challenging as it may seem, it is important to remember that responsibility and answers lie within the patient, and the team serves as her guide and support.

NUTRITIONAL COUNSELING

The following paragraphs offer my philosophy and approach in nutritional counseling, based on three key considerations: physiology, emotion, and behavior.

> *Physiology.* What, why, how much, and when she needs to eat is determined by her nutritional status, such as nutritional deficiency, blood sugar fluctuations, metabolism, weight, and genetics.
>
> *Emotion.* She needs to understand and take responsibility for why and how she turns to, or away from, food to cope with intolerable thoughts and feelings.
>
> *Behavior.* Bingeing, purging, starving, overexercising, using laxatives, diuretics, diet pills, all of which, over time, have become routine ways of managing situations, are destructive, and need to be addressed and exchanged for healthier behaviors.

What expectations can a person struggling with anorexia or bulimia have if she sees a nutritionist? She may feel that it's safer, more acceptable, or she may see the nutritionist as a tool to help reach her ultimate goal: being thin, thinner, or hopefully the thinnest. *My* goal is to get my patients to be able to eat three to five times a day without worrying about their weight, to be able to eat *meals when they are hungry, to stop when they are full,* and *to be able to trust food.* It also involves being free from food obsessions and accepting oneself at a normal body weight. How do I get them to do that or at least try to do that?

A few basic lessons apply, which I will describe here. Beyond that, sessions are adjusted to the patient's individual needs. Any question a patient asks has to be answered in order to reach our goal. What we talk about are the needs of my patients; the number of sessions required for each lesson can and will often vary.

Lesson 1: Daily Caloric Need and Metabolic Rate

At the initial office visit, a personal, family, and nutritional history is taken during which I get to know the patient, her problems, and her goals. The next question is: How can we solve her problems, at least the food-related ones? She is mostly eager to listen and hopeful that I can help her. I explain that, without exercise, the normal average person needs about 1,650 calories per day for metabolism, growth and repair, and maintenance of body temperature and heart and lung function (Satter 1984). With this information, she starts to realize that the body has specific needs and that it does not just store every calorie as fat. The knowledge that the body actually needs about 1,200 calories a day just for metabolism is good news that reassures her when she is ready to resume normal eating again. If the body is underfed—either because of self-starvation or cycles of bingeing/restricting or bingeing/purging—its survival response is to lower its metabolic rate (Keys et al. 1950). How much it will drop depends on the restriction. The patient can recognize this stage because, as the metabolic rate falls, she will experience a decrease in body temperature, muscle tone, and blood-sugar level (Reiff and Reiff 1992). This will make her feel cold, weak, and less able to concentrate. She will get hungry and become preoccupied with food—the body's effort to restore a "normal food intake."

By comparing the effects of different diets, we know that the strictest of them all—starvation—causes weight loss mostly from muscle tissues and very little from fat. Not until one eats a balanced diet of about 1,200 calories per day (1,500 calories for teenagers) and combines it with moderate exercise will one save muscle tissue and lose the weight mostly from fat (Connor and Connor 1986).

After this discussion, the patient has usually grasped what has happened to her. She understands that her metabolism is down and that she cannot eat more—not even normal amounts like her friends—*without first gaining weight*. She feels stuck. The next questions usually come from her: "How can I get my metabolism back up again? Have I ruined it? Is it possible to get it up again?" Luckily the answer is yes, you can get it up again, *but there is a painful price: weight gain!* To better understand the effects of undereating, I often refer to

Martin Katahn's picture in *Beyond Diet*; it has become a helpful educational tool (Katahn 1984) (See Figure 2.1.)

By starting to eat (at least 1,200 calories for females) and doing so until the body "trusts" that this will be the new way of eating, the patient will initially gain weight (Striegel-Moore 1986; Garner and Garfinkel 1984). But after awhile, when the body can depend on this amount of food being available daily, the metabolic rate will increase and eventually the body will burn all calories for its physiological needs (Keys et al. 1950). Because the body now needs more than the minimum 1,200 calories, the food plan becomes a weight-loss plan and the patient starts to lose weight. Understandably this is an exhilarating experience for the patient, which I happily share because she worked hard to get there.

When weight starts to drop, it is important to keep increasing the calories until maintenance is reached. This usually happens between 1,750 and 2,000 calories, the variation depending partly on how active she is.

Consider the following example: A fifteen-year-old girl, who was 5 feet, 6 inches, tall and weighed 116 pounds, came for her initial

Figure 2.1 Metabolic Reactions to a Low-Calorie Diet, by Dr. Martin Katahn

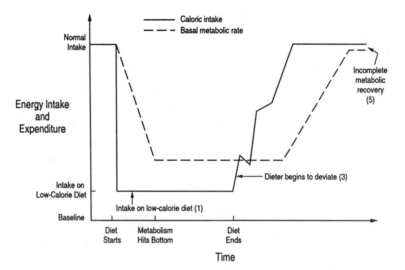

office visit because she had lost 40 pounds in three months. She had had her last period four months earlier. A vegetarian since fourth grade, she was exercising compulsively, consuming no more than 200 calories per day, and was still losing weight. Two weeks later her weight was down to 109 pounds, and she was then hospitalized. Her refeeding was observed by the hospital staff and gradually increased: 1,200 calories, 1,500 calories, 1,800 calories, 2,100 calories, 2,400 calories, and finally 3,600 calories.

The explanation for this refeeding plan is as follows: By consuming 1,200 calories per day she started to gain weight. But after gaining 6 pounds, her metabolism came back up and she maintained her weight. The 1,200 caloric plan then caused her to lose weight and calories had to be increased to 1,500 per day. Since she still lost weight, her intake increased to 1,800 calories per day. She was now able to maintain her weight but had to gain some more in order to qualify for being discharged. Calories were increased to 2,100 per day but her weight was still stable. At 2,400 calories per day she slowly gained weight, but she herself decided to add nutritional fluid supplements to a total of 3,600 calories per day in order to gain enough weight to be discharged. After two months of hospitalization, she was discharged at 126 pounds. To maintain that weight she had to eat 1,800–2,400 calories per day.

When a patient can be treated without hospitalization, a similar but varied program is planned. Patients frequently ask: How long will this take? My answer is always the same: I don't know. We can only guess, but the longer the patient has been trapped with a lowered metabolism, the longer it will likely take to get the metabolism back to normal again. Further, the quicker she gets her calories up to a normal intake, the faster the metabolism will rise. Because we are talking about weeks or maybe a few months, patience is essential. The patient will actually be able to tell me when her metabolism is up because she will experience an increase in energy, a higher body temperature, and a better sleeping pattern, and she will be more physically fit.

By now the patient—although not happy—has an explanation as to why she will need to gain weight. She is now usually eager to work out a food plan. We discuss her short-term goal of eating a minimum of 1,200 calories per day, and her long-term goals of being able to maintain weight on more than 1,700 calories per day. Usually patients feel they want to do everything required in order to get this over and done with, that is, eat 1,200 calories or more right away. Some of them will do that, but some will start lower because they know and feel that this is going to be hard when they get home to their kitchen and try to do this all by themselves.

After having agreed on an acceptable food plan based on the American Dietetic Association's food groups exchange system, the young woman again leaves my office with a handful of food-intake sheets and a new sense of knowledge. She is supposed to use one sheet per day and list when she eats, what she eats, how hungry she was before she ate, and how full she felt after she stopped eating. The heading on the last column reads "feelings." Here she is to write down feelings associated with her eating, either before, during, or after. I will not criticize her for not being able to follow the food plan since most patients cannot do that every day of the week. Instead, I always say that there are no failures, only learning experiences—that is, we need to know what was difficult, why it was difficult, and how we can make it less so. Patients leave with the best intentions to try their hardest, and we try to make the next appointment within the following week.

Lesson 2: Nutritional Assessment and Pubertal Development

Each session usually starts with a quick review of the previous session. Any questions are answered, and we check how the week went by looking at the food-intake sheet. Patients often mention how easy it is to talk about eating while sitting in my office but how hard it is to go home and try to follow the plan. Perhaps the anorexic is motivated while she is in my office, may hear my voice for the first few days after a session, but gradually the fear of gaining weight (or rather fat) becomes overwhelming and she may return to her former controlled way of eating, that is, starvation or semistarvation. If she continues her former eating pattern, she needs to be motivated again. She needs to hear that very few patients are able to begin eating in a balanced way after only one session. To remotivate her, we continue with nutritional assessment—a method where I measure her frame size (small, medium, or large), her upper-arm fatfold and circumference, and her waist fatfold. It is not the most accurate way to assess a patient's nutrition, but it is a valid guideline to learn how her tissues have been affected by starvation.

Referring to these measurements, together we examine the tables, determine her percentage of body fat and muscle tissue, and then compare those figures with the normal expectations for her age and height. When the anorexic patient sees her actual numbers in the tables, more often than not she realizes that her body fat is well below normal, falling in the range of patients who are labeled as underweight or malnourished. She then understands why her periods may no longer be regular. Realizing that her percentage of muscle tissue is below normal disappoints her because now she sees that her recent weight loss has been muscle, not fat. To her, muscle tissue means thighs and arms; she hasn't thought about her weight loss also affecting and shrinking vital organs like her heart, ovaries, and brain. Suddenly realizing how her body has been coping during starvation can be a painful eye-opener. "I didn't know I was hurting myself" is a frequent comment, spoken with fear. In most cases the anorexic patient is now ready to go home and try again, with new food-intake sheets for another week.

The bulimic patient, too, is overwhelmed when she begins the food plan, thinking that keeping all these calories in her system will make her gain weight (i.e., fat). When her fear becomes too burdensome, she is likely to return to her former habit of bingeing and purging. Unlike the anorexic, however, the bulimic patient is less likely to be remotivated by nutritional assessment. Usually she is close to normal weight, but being normal is not good enough for her. She wants to be thin—always thinner than what she is. So with the bulimic patient, instead of nutritional assessment, we spend more time on body image and prevention of binges, which is discussed in a later chapter.

Helpful to both bulimic and anorexic patients is to learn about pubertal development, namely, what happens to the body between the ages of eight and eighteen. A seven-year-old boy and a seven-year-old girl, both nude and viewed from the back, look very much alike. Their percentage of body fat is similar: approximately 18 percent of their total body weight. When these prepubescent children turn eighteen, however, they exhibit a marked difference: The male has either maintained or decreased his body fat by approximately 15 percent, whereas the female has increased her body fat from 18 percent to approximately 28 percent. This occurs over a five-year period, as the female slowly matures to adulthood and is able to bear children. As a pubertal development this all sounds quite logical and acceptable, but it can be quite difficult to deal with as it is occurring. Take, for example, the fifteen-year-old girl who has been away all summer and returns to school in September. She tries on her jeans after the summer and finds them too tight. "Oh," she thinks, "I've gained weight. I'm getting fat. I'd better start a diet so I won't end up looking like Mom or Grandma." When she begins dieting, her goal is to be thin, thinner, she hopes, than before the summer, perhaps even to resemble those models who are thinner than normal, a weight that in reality can be reached by only 2 percent of women without starving or purging. Even though she resents the idea of pubertal development, with its increase in body fat, she is comforted to learn that this is natural, that it happens to us all, and that it doesn't mean she will grow into a fat person. This session is frequently helpful. Accepting ourselves just as we are is not always easy and needs to be addressed over and over again.

Lesson 3: Dehydration Versus Rehydration

We continue reviewing the food-intake sheets during the initial sessions to learn if the food plan is satisfactory, that is, that it doesn't call for too much or too little. If my patient cannot determine this by herself, we check the food groups to see if she was able to eat the minimum daily recommended servings from each food group (two servings from the dairy group, three to six ounces of protein, two servings of vegetables, three fruits, six to seven servings of starches, and four servings of fat). If not, she needs to be remotivated and reminded that *as long as she does not eat the minimum, her metabolism will stay low.*

As difficult as it is for the patient to trust food, she needs to understand that only by eating the minimum will her body get the energy and nutrients it needs for a normal metabolism, maintenance, growth, and body temperature. The minimum intake cannot and will *never* be stored as excess fat, which is what most patients erroneously believe because it feels like that to them. A patient often feels she is gaining fat because refeeding causes the anorexic and bulimic to gain water weight, which causes bloating. Since the anorexic patient is usually dehydrated, a gain of 2–7 pounds over only a weekend is common (Huse and Lucas 1983). The same experience will shock the bulimic when she decides to stop purging (Reiff and Reiff 1992). This seems like a punishment when she is trying so hard to resume normal eating habits. Water retention, the result of low potassium levels because of purging, will remain with the patient for a few weeks until the potassium level, aided by healthier eating, returns to normal.

Rehydration can also occur when someone has been restricting carbohydrate intake, which causes the patient to feel extremely hungry. Then when she eats, she feels guilty.

To help patients respond to this ravenous hunger without feeling as if they are bingeing, it is helpful for them to learn about carbohydrates. Why a lesson to motivate patients to eat carbohydrates? Because, from 1960 to 1980, dieting frequently meant carbohydrate restriction. And it worked. The question was, how? Carbohydrates are stored with water, so by restricting carbohydrates the water weight would drop in big numbers, a loss of 10–15 pounds in two to three weeks. The dieter experienced success, of course, until the former eating habits returned and, with that, an increase in carbohydrates and thus water until all the weight was all gained back, plus 1 extra pound. But the message remained: a diet low in carbohydrates meant lower weight. These dieters would avoid carbohydrates such as bread, pasta, rice, and potatoes, calling them fattening.

With this in mind, it is important to get the facts straight. More than 60 percent of our calories should come from carbohydrates— not only bread, pasta, and rice but also fruits and vegetables (in 1980 the figure had fallen to 43 percent) (Burros 1991). This is our source of energy, and we need it to keep the body systems going. If we do not get enough, which frequently happens with dieters, we experience low blood sugar that results in hunger, headache, and dizziness, sometimes to the point of nausea.

If we wait too long to eat, the body will crave carbohydrates immediately in the form of plain sugar, since that will raise the low blood sugar much more quickly than complex carbohydrates. This is frequently referred to as a *craving for sweets*. If instead we respond to the first hunger signals by eating complex carbohydrates (bread, rice, pasta, and so forth), these cravings for sweets can be minimized.

The person who remains skeptical about converting to a diet high in starch should consider the following: Several years ago, overweight students at Michigan State University each lost an average of 14 pounds after being fed twelve slices of bread a day for eight weeks and instructed to eat whatever else they wanted. More recently, at Hunter College in New York City, students who ate eight slices of bread a day for ten weeks—plus whatever else they wanted—each lost about 9 pounds (Reiff and Reiff 1992). True, students may have been making a special effort to cut back on their food intake to ensure that their weight loss efforts would be successful. But one must take into account that bread, like other starchy foods, has a stick-to-the-ribs quality that satisfies as well as satiates in about twenty minutes. Because complex carbohydrates contain no fat and only 4 calories per gram (fat has 9), complex carbohydrates will also give energy rather than be stored as fat.

Lesson 4: Exercise

It is hoped that use of the food-intake sheets has become a habit by now and that some patients have started to feel comfortable filling in the "feelings" column. We are not referring to all feelings, just those that are food-related—like feeling too full, being aware of not eating enough, or experiencing guilt over bingeing or purging.

At this stage in treatment, exercise should be discussed, especially if the patient is bulimic or a compulsive overeater. Why do we need to exercise? How often and how much exercise is necessary to stay healthy? Because the eating-disordered patient tends to be a compulsive exerciser, what is normal and how much exercise is needed for weight loss needs to be established. In order to have a body—or specifically, a heart—that is at the same biological age as one's numerical age, one needs to exercise aerobically three to four times a week for thirty to forty minutes (Bernardot 1992). For weight loss, exercising five to seven times a week for forty-five to sixty minutes has been recommended. I discuss exercise with the patient because it can help her feel better about herself. If she is not exercising enough, she will in most cases feel healthier by increasing her physical activity to a normal level. If she is exercising too much, she needs to realize that she is using exercise as a way of purging, and this behavior should be addressed.

Lesson 5: Prevention of Bingeing/Purging

By the fifth lesson, the patient has usually realized that the way she used to treat her body was self-destructive. She understands how her body coped during starvation or during episodes of bingeing and possibly also purging. But knowing is one thing and doing something about it another. I have frequently heard: "I feel motivated to change my habits. I realize I have to eat—it is the only way out—but I just cannot get myself to do it. This self-destructive behavior has become the only way I know to take care of myself that feels safe."

At this point the nutritional therapist needs to tune in to the struggling patient in her efforts to eat. By changing the food plan according to what she can handle for the time being, she will feel listened to and accepted. The anorexic patient may be more likely to try harder if the recommended intake is reduced, and the bulimic or compulsive overeater may want it reduced or increased, depending on her earlier habits. After the adjustment has been made and she feels somewhat more comfortable with the suggested food plan, she is ready to try again. If it is still too difficult, the reason for not being able to follow the food plan should be addressed. This may be done by asking four consecutive questions:

1. What is going on?
2. How does that make you feel?
3. Does eating help? Does it solve the problems?
4. What can you do instead?

With the first question the patient has to open up to a situation or an incident that recently had an effect on her, like "My boyfriend did not call" or "My father expects me to get an A on my math test" or "My poor mother, she is so unhappy." To answer the next question—"How do you feel about that?"—I show her a list (vocabulary of feelings) containing one hundred feelings typed in alphabetical order. She is surprised that there are so many feelings. I now ask her to highlight the ones that describe her mood. This makes her feel slightly better, not only because I can now empathize with her since I know how she feels but also because she herself has a name for these uncomfortable feelings. Patients are often elated to find a vocabulary that finally describes what they have been coping with.

The third question has two parts. There is a short-term question: Does restricting or eating help? Does it make you feel better? In most cases, the answer is yes! Not everyone knows why but, after some thought, most patients admit that restricting or eating numbs those painful feelings they just realized they had had. We call that *emotional* restricting or eating, as opposed to *physical* eating, which is when we eat because of hunger. The second part of this question deals with the long-term picture: Does restricting or eating solve the problem? We agree that it does not, so now she needs to address the last question: What can I do instead of restricting or eating? It is hoped that appropriate brainstorming will lead to suggestions about what to do. Deep down, filled with fear, the anorexic knows that she needs to eat and face her blocked feelings. For the bulimic and the compulsive overeater, suggestions might include exercising, attacking a long-awaited project (cleaning a closet), calling someone, writing about it, or just accepting it. In order to "just accept it," patients have found it helpful to analyze realistically the situation that caused the feelings. This analysis helps the patient realize that her feelings are frequently based on personal assumptions about what others would think or say about her—rather than reality.

The patient eventually will become somewhat aware of these new, often painful feelings that can be overwhelming and try to get in touch with them. The therapist and nutritionist will communicate with each other regarding focus and content in order to coordinate this part of emotional relearning. Learning how to deal with new feelings frequently leads to continuous restriction or binge eating. The patient comes to realize slowly how she unconsciously has been responding to mental discomfort. She is now more ready than ever to listen to suggestions on prevention. How can she help herself not to eat or overeat/binge over emotional issues? After some brainstorming, anything is worthwhile practicing. With the bulimic patient who binges, it may be helpful to plan strategy, that is, behavior modification.

Lesson 6: Hunger

Hunger is experienced as something scary and therefore needs to be addressed frequently. What, then, is hunger? Is it safe? Can I trust it? For many people it is the enemy. Some would call it thin guilt: a painful reminder that one does not deserve food. All this may lead to a discussion about the strength of self: *How long can I make it without food?*

Personally I love hunger. It is a safe signal that tells me that whatever I ate earlier has now been used up. Every single calorie has been used for bodily functions like metabolism, body temperature, or perhaps maintenance and growth. I do not know exactly what the calories were used for, but I know that they were not stored as fat and that it is my responsibility to nourish my body again, now that it has told me through its hunger that it needs to be refueled.

If we only ate when we were hungry, we would have nothing to fear. Only when we eat when we are not hungry (because of habitual or emotional eating) do we get more than we need and the excess is stored as fat. "But what if I eat too much when I am hungry?" I am asked. How often have we said: "Why did I eat so much?" It is difficult to know just when the body has had enough and is satisfied—especially after restriction, when the body seems to have an insatiable hunger. "When should I stop eating?" I am asked. "Just how should it feel when we have reached physiological satiety?" I answer in the following way: This is something that takes practice and experience, and we each have to learn our own levels of satiety. It should be a comfortable feeling and give us a sense of control. *But it does not really matter if you underate or overate as long as you respond appropriately to hunger the next time it comes.* In other words, if you overate, your body is likely to get hungrier later, and therefore you should wait and eat no sooner than when you are hungry again. This could be an hour or two later than you had planned. When the body is physiologically hungry it is letting you know that it has used up all the calories for physiological needs. It is when we respond to hunger in a natural way—by eating (or we might call it refueling)—that the metabolism will function and burn calories at an optimal level. If one eats before one is hungry (maybe because of an emotional reason), all the calories are not used up and the excess has to go somewhere. Thus it may be stored as fat! On the other hand, if one undereats or has been restricting, one's body becomes hungry again very soon after eating, maybe only one hour or even half an hour after eating.

Sometimes a patient describes a situation in which she was not hungry when she started eating, but, by forcing herself to eat, hunger came in strongly and she then could not stop eating. There are also patients who, instead of undereating, find themselves hungrier than the prescribed meal plan. When one who has restricted food intake finally acknowledges hunger, it starts to come in first like a lamb, but then as a ravenous lion. This is frightening to a patient who fears that this is only the beginning of an insatiable hunger. The patient may believe that this is how hungry she will always be. Because it feels as though she could eat 10,000 calories, she thinks she will surely eat herself into fatness, an unacceptable thought that makes her feel out of control.

The reality is that after the starvation, when the patient eventually decides to try to eat again, her body is finally able to send hunger signals that are now experienced and not, as before, denied. The body sends these signals to make up for the loss of essential body tissues during the early starvation. If the patient dares to respond to these hunger feelings by eating more, her body will get what it needs to reach a normal body weight and will stop being overly hungry. This hunger will and can only turn into satiety if the food she is eating contains enough fat. Fat intake below the minimal daily requirement (20 grams) leads to fat phobia and symptoms like dry skin and hair, cold intolerance, and irregular menses. With the recent introduction of many low-fat and no-fat products and the general consensus that fat is bad for you, the eating disordered patient thinks she is healthy by eating less than the minimum daily requirement. After consuming a low-fat meal, she will feel hungry again after only one to two hours.

A balanced intake is of great importance and with a fat intake of 40–60 grams distributed over three meals, which is still considered *low fat* (normal being 80–120 grams of fat per day), the patient can now enjoy full satiety between meals. By accepting this instruction and allowing herself to consume a *low-fat* or *normal-fat* intake, she can resume a pre-eating disorder state, that is, normal hunger will be felt at regular intervals and she will be able to eat what normal people are eating.

Dan W. Reiff's graphic descriptions of these various hunger patterns are illustrated in Figures 2.2, 2.3, and 2.4. This visual representation of hunger is most helpful for the eating-disordered patient because it describes where she is and what her goal should be. The typical hunger and food-intake pattern of a person who has recovered is what a young woman, who eventually responds to her body's signals of hunger, will experience when she starts to trust hunger. Finally, what she has been longing and waiting for has become a reality: She is at her normal weight, she eats when she is hungry, and her weight is stable. A "healthy control" becomes a reality, and she eventually trusts that she can reach the ultimate goal: *to eat when one is hungry; to stop whenever one decides one feels full; and, in between, not to worry, obsess, or think about food.*

Lesson 7: The Effect of PMS

Having an eating disorder can be extremely frustrating. Such a person is often torn between trying to help herself get better by eating and trying to lose weight to maintain control. She therefore needs to feel empathy from a treatment team she can trust. She needs to understand what has happened to her body in order to be motivated to get better. One of the last obstacles to confront her in her struggle to eat better is PMS (premenstrual syndrome). PMS affects about 40 percent of today's women for as many as ten days to only a few before their menstrual period. Most of those women affected feel bloated, moody, fatigued, headachy, and frequently fat. The experienced "bloat" is the result of water retention that can vary from one to seven pounds. It can be identified by tight rings on a swollen hand. The increased moodiness is thought to be related to hormonal changes; the afflicted patient frequently describes it as going from seeing the glass half-full to seeing it half-empty. It is also a time when the patient may regress in her treatment, that is, she's viewing herself more positively and realistically but then PMS strikes and she again is questioning and criticizing

Figure 2.2 Typical Hunger and Food Intake Pattern of Person Who Has Recovered, by Dan W. Reiff, MPH, RD

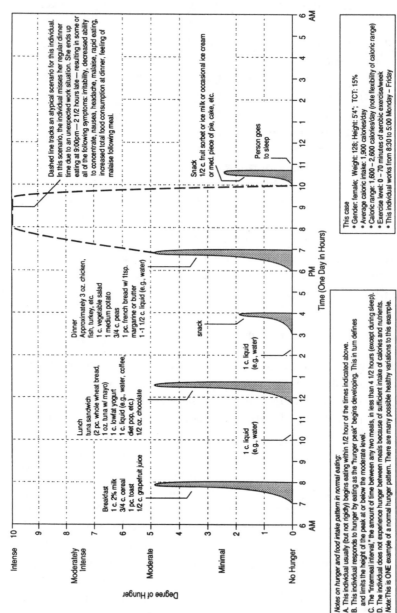

Notes on hunger and food intake pattern in normal eating:
A. This individual usually (but not nightly) begins eating within 1/2 hour of the times indicated above.
B. This individual responds to hunger by eating as the "hunger peak" begins developing. This in turn defines and limits the height of the peak at or below the moderate level.
C. The "internal interval," the amount of time between any two meals, in less than 4 1/2 hours (except during sleep).
D. The individual does not experience hunger between meals because of sufficient intake of calories and nutrients.
Note: This is ONE example of a normal hunger pattern. There are many possible healthy variations to this example.

This case
• Gender: female; Weight: 128; Height: 5'4"; TCT: 15%
• Average caloric intake: 1,900 calories/day
• Caloric range: 1,600 – 2,600 calories/day (note flexibility of caloric range)
• Exercise level: 0 – 70 minutes of aerobic exercise/week
• This individual works from 8:30 to 5:00 Monday – Friday

Figure 2.3 Typical Hunger and Food Intake Pattern of Person Who Has Anorexia Nervosa, by Dan W. Reiff, MPH, RD

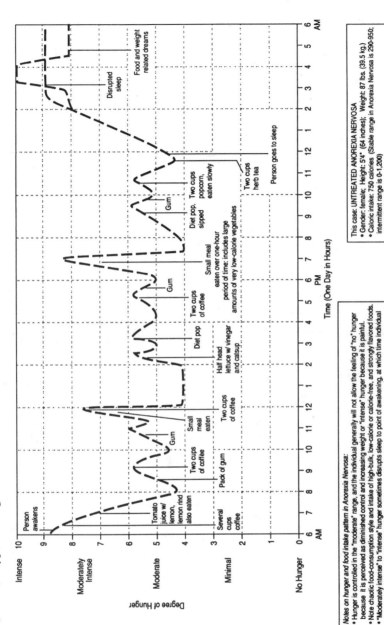

This case: UNTREATED ANOREXIA NERVOSA
• Gender: female; Height: 5'4" (64 inches); Weight: 87 lbs. (39.5 kg.)
• Caloric intake: 750 calories (Stable range in Anorexia Nervosa is 290-950; intermittent range is 0-1,200)
• Exercise level: None

Notes on hunger and food intake pattern in Anorexia Nervosa:
• Hunger is controlled in the "moderate" range, and the individual generally will not allow the feeling of "no" hunger because it is perceived as diminished control and increasing weight or "intense" hunger because it is painful.
• Note chaotic food-consumption style and intake of high-bulk, low-calorie or calorie-free, and strongly flavored foods.
• "Moderately intense" to "intense" hunger sometimes disrupts sleep to point of awakening, at which time individual may use food or exercise behavior.
• Food dreams are typical during "moderately intense" to "intense" hunger phases.

Figure 2.4 Typical Hunger and Food Intake Pattern of Person Who Has Bulimia Nervosa, by Dan W. Reiff, MPH, RD

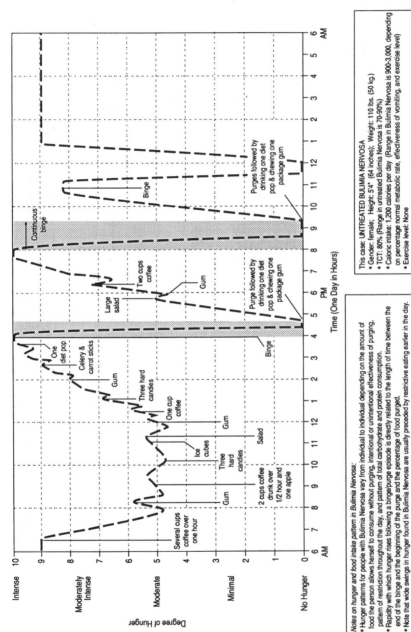

Notes on hunger and food intake pattern in Bulimia Nervosa:
• Hunger patterns for people with Bulimia Nervosa vary from individual to individual depending on the amount of food the person allows herself to consume without purging, intentional or unintentional effectiveness of purging, pattern of restriction throughout the day, and pattern of total carbohydrate and protein consumption.
• Rapidity with which hunger rises following a binge/purge episode is directly related to the length of time between the end of the binge and the beginning of the purge and the percentage of food purged.
• Note that wide swings in hunger found in Bulimia Nervosa are usually preceded by restrictive eating earlier in the day.

This case: UNTREATED BULIMIA NERVOSA
• Gender: female; Height: 5'4" (64 inches); Weight: 110 lbs. (50 kg.)
• TCT: 80% (Range in untreated Bulimia Nervosa is 70-90%)
• Caloric intake: 1,200 calories per day (Range in Bulimia Nervosa is 900-3,000, depending on percentage normal metabolic rate, effectiveness of vomiting, and exercise level)
• Exercise level: None

herself. She frequently feels hopeless ("I will never be able to overcome this eating disorder"). She experiences an increased need for sleep and rest but rarely allows herself the luxury of listening to her body's signals; sometimes she mixes up the need for sleep, thinking that by eating more she will have more energy to help her get through the end of the day. Even worse, water retention during PMS makes her feel fat. This immediately sends a message to her: "Gain control and lose weight." At the same time, the body has an increased caloric need of about 200–350 calories a day (Wurtman 1989). Rather than listen to her increased hunger signal, she tries to restrict herself and eat less—but then she pays a price. Because she is not providing her body with the extra needed calories from complex carbohydrates, later in the day her body starts craving plain sugar. (Her body does not have the time to wait for complex carbohydrates to break down into simple sugars, so now it demands pure sugar instead.) This scares both the anorexic and the bulimic patient. At a time when the bulimic patient thought she might be over the hurdle and promised herself never to binge again, a PMS sugar craving may lead to one last binge. Again, it is important to listen to the body's signals—they are there for a reason; by listening to them and responding with the appropriate action during this more difficult time (i.e., eating 200–350 calories extra a day, mainly from complex carbohydrates), peace will follow. About three days after menstruation the water retention is gone, and she returns to her premenstrual weight.

Lesson 8: Expectations

Other matters need to be addressed in nutritional counseling, but some issues may be adjusted to the patient's knowledge, such as lessons about proteins, fats, processed foods, vegetarian combinations, eating out in restaurants, foods in social situations (particularly during holidays), food myths, and so forth. No specific timing is assigned to these issues. Rather, questions or problems should be addressed when they arise.

Of great importance is that expectations remain realistic. When a concern is mentioned in counseling, the patient has to allow herself enough time to master the problem fully. For example, before she can stop herself from eating for emotional reasons, she must accept that *emotional eating* indeed exists. Then she has to decide whether this applies to her and, if so, does she want to work on it. Only then are we ready to suggest how she might separate emotional eating from physical eating. Eventually she is ready to practice not responding to an emotional situation by eating. After a sufficient amount of practice, we wait for the behavior to become habitual, at which time no further work is needed. In other words, the patient must be allowed enough time from when the problem first comes up, to the patient's accepting it, to trying different solutions, to practicing what seems to work best, and, finally, to getting the problem under control. Frequently these girls are perfectionists and think they can master the problem immediately. That this process takes time bears repeating when patients who cannot succeed on their first try view their effort as a failure rather than as a learning experience.

The recognition that time is essential is of great importance for both the anorexic and bulimic patient but perhaps even more so for the compulsive overeater, who feels that all she has ever done was to fail any diet she tried. Low-calorie diets are a setup for binges and continued weight gain and should no longer be allowed. Instead, based on her hunger, she needs to learn how much she can eat to maintain her weight since she usually has either been gaining or losing weight. When she is comfortable and trusts her maintenance plan, prevention of binges and increased activity is usually enough to help her lose weight. Further, after losing 10 percent of her body weight, she needs to maintain that weight for a few weeks in order to prove to herself that she is in control and is capable of maintaining her weight.

I have found that a crucial element of successful treatment has been to adjust to the patient's pace, if possible. Of course this is not possible when a patient is severely underweight, in critical condition, and must be forced to eat beyond her own perceived capacity. With that one exception, the therapist needs to be sensitive to the patient's apprehensions and, with compliments and positive reinforcement, to understand and support her through her struggle. The patient must be able to trust her nutritional counselor whose task it is to help her restore her normal weight—the very thing the patient fears most.

Lesson 9. Realistic Body Weight and Body Image

There is a difference between ideal body weight and preferred body weight, and this can only be discussed when the patient is ready to do so. Most likely, discussion can only occur when she has accepted her weight gain from rehydration.

Initially the patient's preferred body weight resembles that of her thin role models who are about 5 feet, 10 inches, and weigh about 110 pounds. In order to remain so thin, most of us would have to deny our hunger, deprive ourselves of what our bodies need, and probably obsess about food day and night. One would think that no one would choose to suffer through something like that. But because being thin today is frequently associated with being successful, living a better life, and being in control, it is not surprising that so many are willing to pay this price to get thin.

Today, depending on which survey one looks at, 70 percent to nearly 90 percent of women report dissatisfaction with their bodies and a desire to lose weight. In fact, body hatred is not about our bodies at all, but about self-doubt and feelings of inadequacy. Focusing on perceived body faults and not dealing with our real struggles and unpleasant feelings becomes a convenient scapegoat. This is why it is so difficult for the anorexic patient to gain weight. She focuses on feeling fat—her distorted body image—when in reality she is emaciated. I generally guide any patient who says "I feel fat" to change her focus by rephrasing her feeling to "I feel inadequate, because . . ."

By regaining weight, her disturbed body image will not totally change but it will improve. But how much must she gain? A realistic body weight refers to a genetically determined amount of body fat that the body actively defends. This is frequently referred to as the set-point weight (Reiff and Reiff 1992). The body acts in such a way as to maintain this weight range and, if it is challenged, will defend it vigorously by altering metabolic rate and intensity of hunger. The following sums it up succinctly: set-point weight is the weight a person's body maintains within a few pounds (3–5) when the individual is not thinking about it. A patient who is maintaining a weight below her genetically or biologically predetermined set-point will know it because of an increased obsession with food, weight, and hunger. Recovery should require not only attaining a minimum critical weight range but ultimately allowing weight to reach the set-point range.

Only by eating will the patient stop obsessing about food and gain enough energy to move from self-doubt to self-acceptance. Consider the following cases.

Case 1

Lisa had been bulimic for about five years when she came to treatment. The eating disorder started with anorexia in college where she lost quite a lot of weight. She soon realized that in order to maintain her lower body weight she could not eat anything, or, if she did, she had to purge. After graduation she was confused and did not know what to do; the bulimia got worse. She never told anyone, but finally the guilt became so difficult to bear that she had to do something about it. So, on her own, she came to the Wilkins Center, severely depressed, withdrawn (she had dropped all her friends), and nutritionally starved. At this time Lisa purged by vomiting once or twice a day, and she constantly obsessed about food. "What am I going to eat tonight, when am I going to eat it, and how much can I eat" were questions she frequently asked herself. She also took laxatives and diet pills but not to a great extent. She might have taken a double dosage, but she never took a whole box. Her immediate treatment plan suggested medical visits, nutritional counseling, and individual as well as group therapy. She committed herself to everything except group therapy, for she was too embarrassed to participate in a group; she could not even say the word bulimia, but she was relieved to know she was not alone in her suffering.

"Annika put up with a lot seeing me," Lisa would say later. "I would just go in and cry, which was partly physical because I was so hungry and so starved and weak and I did not know how to eat properly. I was not getting any nutrition, so no wonder I did not feel well."

Lisa was a difficult patient because it was hard for her to accept that her metabolic rate had dropped because of starvation and that now she had to eat normally in order to increase her metabolism. That meant a weight gain, later followed by learning maintenance eating, and eventually losing weight (with the metabolic rate still up) to an acceptable level.

We gradually increased the calories and Lisa started to gain weight—for her, quite a lot. She did not eat all that was listed on her food plan and still she gained 15 pounds, which was very scary for her! What she absolutely hated was to get on the scale. It would ruin her whole day and give us a good reason to start dealing with this very hot issue.

By this time Lisa was no longer underweight. Physically she started feeling better, but her clothes did not fit. She realized that in the long run it was better for her to normalize her weight and her eating. To do so she needed frequent reminders, motivation, and support, so she increased the frequency of her sessions to twice a week. As Lisa improved nutritionally, her bulimia improved and became less intense; her physical craving for food diminished. Still, she did not have total control. By increasing her awareness of her emotional life, she began to realize how bingeing took the place of dealing with upsetting situations. After much practice, she was able to label these situations and her accompanying feelings, and realize that under no circumstances would eating solve her problems. Eating might temporarily numb her emotional discomfort, but it would never help get rid of it. Thus she recognized the importance of separating eating from feelings: Eating is what we do when we are hungry; overwhelming feelings have to be acknowledged and brought into therapy in order to bring peace or resolution.

Because eating to numb uncomfortable feelings had been a bad habit for more than five years, we had to come up with activities that Lisa could do when she felt the urge to binge—a "substitute list." In the beginning she said, "It sounds stupid and like a waste of time," but the list assisted her in many ways. Even the slightest act of brushing her teeth helped, because, afterward, she did not feel like putting food in her mouth for at least an hour, enough time to prevent her from bingeing.

Other coping ideas on Lisa's list were going out for a walk, listening to music, and drinking a large glassful of water to help her feel full. In addition, Lisa would continually talk to herself about her long-term goal—to stop purging! If she binged without purging, her calorie intake would be excessive and that bothered her. All this helped her to gain control.

Finally, Lisa agreed to try group therapy. She was embarrassed initially and had difficulty even looking at anyone. But group therapy was helpful in the end—she made friends and finally felt comfortable talking about her problems. She is now totally recovered, married, and has one child. She was happy to have been able to eat normally throughout her pregnancy. Some foods may still feel frightening to Lisa, but she is probably using good sense not to eat them. For instance, she has no trouble eating an ice-cream cone, but she will forego an ice-cream sundae because the sauce would be an absolute waste of calories.

She is once again socially active, going to parties, out to dinner, or any other place where food is served. She is no longer preoccupied or worried about how to handle food.

Nutritional counseling played an important part in Lisa's recovery, which she reached only after much hard work. Having different people involved in her treatment made her feel special. She felt she was getting both individualized attention as well as working together with her counselors as a family, where communication was open and necessary. As she said: "It wasn't like seeing three different people. It was like seeing one Center."

Case 2

Sue developed an eating disorder when she was seventeen and had just moved back to the United States from Australia, where she and her family had lived for a few years. Several events triggered the onset: First, she went to a camp where she had a difficult time making friends because of an accident that prevented her from taking part in camp activities. Second, when she entered tenth grade she did not fit in. Sue was not prepared to be a private-school student, dressed in nice-looking clothes and uniforms. She felt as if she were betraying her friends in Australia, who favored black and punk clothing. In truth, Sue hadn't wanted to leave Australia and didn't try to make friends after she moved. Third, within the next three months her grandmother and great-uncle died, and Sue had been very close to both. To Sue, life was out of control; the only way to get it under control was to go on a diet. Thinness to her was a sign of being "all together"—at least on the outside. She started out by following a plan of what she would eat every day and what exercises she would do. When she was unhappy she would be more restrictive, and then she became obsessive. After two to three hours of basketball practice, she would return home and ride an exercise bike for an hour, then do sit-ups and another two hours of exercise. Finally, she had to skip meals, starting with dinner, then lunch. Sometimes she got away with eliminating breakfast, too. She was able to get away with this behavior because her father was traveling a lot and her mom at the time was preoccupied with taking care of her recently widowed grandfather. For a while it was just Sue and her brother. He was two years older but was never social, so Sue was always the one to be counted on—"the best little girl in the world" (Levenkron 1979), the reliable one. Her parents, therefore, never thought to worry that something might happen to her. Finally, Sue realized that she could not keep up with all the exercising and starvation, so she began to eat and throw up. She knew from the beginning that what she was doing was self-destructive, but she couldn't stop it.

Sue thought that technically she didn't binge, because for her a binge meant consuming perhaps 3,000 calories. When she learned that a binge could be any amount of food that is overwhelming for a person to eat, even a tenth of a sandwich, she realized she was bulimic. Any amount of food she ate, no matter what it was, would cause her to panic and get rid of it. Throwing up made her feel awful, so she would exercise for an hour. Sue was able to keep her behavior a secret for about five months by using lots of little tricks; eventually, though, she couldn't take it anymore and told her parents.

Sue had been afraid to reveal herself to her parents because she had always been concerned with what they would think of her. She was trying to live up to their expectations. She didn't want to disappoint them, especially since they felt that, compared to her brother, "Sue really has it together; she is losing weight and she looks wonderful." At first she did have it together. She got wonderful grades; so, as far as they could tell, they had the "perfect kid"— which is just what Sue wanted to be, and thought she was—at least on the outside.

What she was really thinking was worse. She thought that if she was skinny she would have more friends and boyfriends. Everything would be perfect. But the pressure only made things much worse than they had ever been before. She realized that her self-esteem had plummeted so much that she was incapable of helping herself. What triggered her to speak up was that her cousin—a social worker—had figured out what was going on and showed her scary pictures of a relative who had been anorexic and bulimic since she was fifteen.

Feeling totally out of control, she realized she needed help and agreed to meet with Dr. Diane Mickley, the internist and director of the Wilkins Center, who recommended individual therapy and nutritional counseling.

Sue was ready for treatment, and after our first nutritional meeting she stopped purging (vomiting). She wanted to believe that if she ate a balanced diet she could be healthy and active and wouldn't have to end up obese. She knew she had a lot to learn and that this was how she was going to help herself get better—by her own choice.

It meant a lot for Sue to find a role model in me, her dietitian. She liked me to show her that this was all possible, but she needed to be frequently reassured and remotivated. Sue's eating patterns were messed up; she didn't know what a portion was and needed redefinition of normal serving sizes. By learning how many calories her body needed daily, and why, and what would happen if it didn't get these calories, she began to accept eating as a way of getting better. Like other patients, Sue needed help dealing with the weight she gained back. She had lost 35 pounds, which caused her to stop menstruating and to grow fine hair on her face and body. She had lost some hair on her head, and her skin was pale and extremely dry. She looked unhealthy and emaciated but still thought she looked fat—she also felt fat, although she could count her ribs.

In initiating normal eating Sue had a choice: to begin immediately eating three normal meals a day (a full-fledged normal eating pattern) or, if that was too scary, to increase her food intake gradually. Like most patients she chose the gradual route. The very slow start prompted her parents to comment that "not even a mouse could survive on that." Everyone involved understood that eating was Sue's own responsibility. She was not going to eat for me, for her parents, or for her teachers—only for herself and her own needs. Therefore we had asked all those involved to leave it up to Sue and not make it more difficult with comments or even looks.

As Sue gained weight, every single pound scared her. She went through phases where she would eat normally and not exercise at all, or restrict her eating and exercise a lot, so we had weight fluctuations throughout the recovering period. This happened three times during the refeeding phase. The first occurrence was when Sue initially stopped purging and starving and gradually started to eat, immediately gaining five pounds, mostly in water weight. (Normally patients gain from 2 to 7 pounds within the first week or two.) In a couple of weeks this bloatedness was gone. The second time Sue experienced weight fluctuations was when she stopped denying the hunger. This immense body signal was overwhelming for Sue since she felt that responding to it would result in overeating to the point of becoming overweight. Instead she began to restrict again and lost a few pounds. With remotivation she was again able to gain weight. Sue's third and last struggle with the scale was when she approached 100 pounds. Being below 100 pounds meant being special: She felt strong. She could count her ribs, a wonderful sign of success. When the scale tipped slightly above 100 pounds, she felt she was no longer special, that she weighed just what everyone else weighs. So again she began to restrict her intake and exercise a lot.

What came to be most important for Sue was her ability (in our sessions) to see how her thinking was distorted and how she was able to turn it around to being realistic. This helped her be happier with herself. For example, if her mom told her that she had to have dinner, she would get scared for a moment and react: "No, she cannot make me eat! I am bigger than she is. She cannot make me do this, she is shorter than I am. She cannot force-feed me!" Then she would feel strong. She would also tell herself, on seeing someone eating cake, for example, that that person was weak, that she herself was strong by not eating that cake. She would make similar comments about any other foods that she used to eat and that now were forbidden to her. At her very first visit Dr. Mickley told her, "When you are happy it doesn't matter how much you weigh." Sue couldn't believe her ears; she thought Dr. Mickley must be crazy! It was the stupidest remark she had ever heard; but if one were to ask her how she feels today, she would tell you she's never been happier and honestly doesn't know how much she weighs.

Sue had thought that if she were thin she would have everything she wanted, like friends and boyfriends. But she eventually realized that people would like her only if she learned to like herself. During her anorexic-bulimic months, she did not like herself and did not attract any people. That is why she listened and was open for a change. For example, she would tell me, "Oh well, you know, I was really bad. I had a scoop of ice cream and some cookies." She was frightened by her behavior. By realizing that this was normal behavior and that she didn't need to feel she was "bad," she was slowly able to practice more positive thinking.

In contrast to others, Sue did not accomplish much in individual psychotherapy; she disliked herself too much to disclose personal information. To avoid discussing herself, she would talk about family issues or other matters, thus making limited use of therapy.

By changing her eating behavior, Sue started to feel better physically. Her food obsessions and cravings decreased tremendously, and she had more time and energy to devote to other aspects of life. She joined a hot line to help others like herself who were suffering from eating disorders. She found that it also helped her to be open about her experience. Now, on a board of directors with adults whom she doesn't know very well, she can speak with confidence. She has made new friends from the hot line, people who also had problems and were able to talk with her about them. During their many conversations, Sue learned who they thought she was and gradually her understanding of herself grew.

Another area where Sue needed help was with her body image—the last distortion to be given up if one has had an eating disorder. When she was underweight she felt fat, even though, as I've indicated, she was able to count her ribs. Because she admired my body composition, she weighed me, measured my height, and discovered that I weighed more than two pounds per inch. When, together, we compared this to her own measurements, which were 1.7 pounds per inch, she again had to face reality. She felt bigger and fatter than I but had to admit that she, in fact, was considerably thinner. When we looked at the numbers from the nutritional assessment, they showed that since Sue had lost all the body fat she possibly could, her body had coped with her starvation by breaking down muscular tissue to the point where she qualified as being not just underweight but malnourished. This was a shock to Sue and motivated her to eat more, gain weight, and bring her weight up to normal—without being overweight, her constant fear.

While she was slowly gaining weight, she had to be assured that she wasn't overweight, so on a few occasions we spent time repeating the nutritional assessment. This always reassured her since it allowed her to follow her body signals: to eat because her body needed food to function.

As Sue recovered she weighed 160 pounds at a height of 5 feet, 10 inches. Even though she was fixated with the numbers on the scale and would have liked to lose ten pounds, she was not going to starve herself to achieve it. Instead, she realized that people have a certain body weight that is right for them; because she liked the way she looked, she gave up fighting the numbers on the scale. The real accomplishment was that she did not feel bad about herself for not losing those ten pounds. In other words, she no longer had to be 100 percent perfect.

What truly benefited Sue was her motivation to reach her goal: to be happy, to exercise normally, and to look good. She trusted me and used me as a role model. I was able to show her that her goal was possible once she turned her negative critical thinking into positive and rewarding thinking. She finally learned to like herself because of *who* she is—not because of how thin she is!

Preventing abnormal eating patterns is not an easy task. It represents a unique and unusual challenge for the dietitian who needs to have an understanding of the psychodynamics of eating disorders. This insight will help the dietitian build a relationship based on evolving trust, a necessary ingredient if the patient is to feel safe and motivated to meet challenges on her road to recovery.

These, then, are the ways in which I implement recovery. They are specific to eating-disordered patients but may be seen as basic concepts in eating for good health and a sense of well-being, with mind and body functioning smoothly in response to the ever present dynamic interplay that represents our body as a whole.

References

American Dietetic Association. 1988. Position of the American Dietetic Association. "Nutrition Intervention in the Treatment of Anorexia Nervosa and Bulimia Nervosa and Binge Eating." *Journal of the American Dietetic Association* 4, no. 8 (August 1994): 902–7.

Andersen, A. 1988. "Medical Consequences and Complications of the Eating Disordered." *Directions in Psychiatry* 8, Lesson 10: 3–7.

Bayer, L., C. M. Bauers, and S. K. Kapp. 1983. "Psychosocial Aspects of Nutritional Support." *Nursing Clinics of North America* 18, no. 1: 119–28.

Bernardot, D., ed. 1992. *Sports Nutrition: A Guide for the Professional Working with Active People*. In-house publication of the American Dietetic Association.

Burros, M. 1991. "Eating Well: Carbohydrates Are Dieter's Best Friend." Living Section, C1, *New York Times*, March 6.

Connor, S., and W. Connor. 1986. *The New American Diet*. New York: Simon and Schuster.

Garner, D., and P. E. Garfinkel. 1984. "Psychoeducational Principles in the Treatment of Bulimia and Anorexia Nervosa." In *Handbook of Psychotherapy for Anorexia Nervosa and Bulimia*. New York: Guilford.

Huse, C. D., and A. Lucas. 1983. "Dietary Treatment of Anorexia Nervosa." *Perspectives in Practice* 83, no. 6.

Johnson, C., and M. Connors. 1982. *The Etiology and Treatment of Bulimia Nervosa*. New York: Basic Books.

Katahn, M. 1984. *Beyond Diet*. New York: Norton.

Keys, A., J. Brozek, A. Henschel, O. Mickelsen, and H. L. Taylor. 1950. *The Biology of Human Starvation*. Minneapolis: University of Minnesota Press. Summarized in F. Berg, "Effects of Human Starvation." *Obesity and Health* (January/February 1993): 12–15.

Levenkron, S. 1979. *The Best Little Girl in the World*. New York: Warner.

Reiff, D., and K. Reiff. 1992. *Eating Disorders: Nutrition Therapy in the Recovery Process*. Gaithersburg, Md.: Aspen.

Satter, E. 1984. *Child of Mine: Feeding with Love and Good Sense*. New York: Bull.

Striegel-Moore, R. 1986. "Toward an Understanding of Risk Factors for Bulimia." *American Psychologist* 41, no. 3: 246–63.

Wurtman, J. 1989. "Carbohydrate Therapy for Premenstrual Syndrome." *American Journal of Obstetrics and Gynecology* 161:1228.

Psychiatric Consultation with Eating Disordered Patients

DAVID GREENFELD

Psychiatric consultation may play an important role in the evaluation and treatment of many patients with eating disorders. Any clinician working with eating disordered patients quickly becomes aware that the range and intensity of their symptoms and eating behaviors vary widely. A psychiatric consultation may be indicated for those patients whose symptoms are persistent or severe, whose clinical presentations are complicated or atypical, who present with symptoms of other disorders along with their eating symptoms, or who fail to respond to conservative management. The consultation can help to clarify diagnostic questions and may help to guide the treatment more effectively. In some instances the consultation can result in the prescription of medication that can advance the treatment.

Patients and families may be hesitant to consult with a psychiatrist. They may be fearful that the referral is an indication that the eating disorder is extremely serious or that the patient is suffering from some additional serious mental illness. Sometimes that may indeed be the case because the patient's symptoms are more serious or more resistant to treatment. However, as noted above, for others the referral is often not so much because the clinician feels the patient is deeply disturbed but because of a sense that the patient's problems are in some ways puzzling and difficult, and that another perspective may be useful. The psychiatric consultant may provide this new perspective in a single consultation or may become a member of the treatment team, prescribing and adjusting the dose of medications that help to relieve symptoms and speed recovery. It is important to recognize that the psychiatric consultant will not supplant the primary clinician nor control the treatment's overall direction. The consultant gives advice and makes recommendations in collaboration with the other members of the treatment team, but final responsibility for the patient must rest with the primary clinician.

Even in comparatively uncomplicated eating disordered patients, psychiatric consultation may play a useful role. This is particularly true for patients suffering from bulimia. Substantial research evidence and much clinical experience has demonstrated that many (but not all) bulimic patients are helped by treatment with antidepressant medication. It is not clear why this should be so, and it does not mean that bulimic patients who respond to the antidepressants are clinically depressed. Even in those patients who have no depressive symptoms, the antidepressants often reduce the intensity and frequency of urges to binge and purge. It is important to understand that the medication is *at best* a useful adjunct to treatment and, most emphatically, is *not* a substitute for counseling. Indeed, it is quite rare for the medication to produce a complete remission of symptoms, but the reduction of impulses to binge and purge can give a needed boost to the psychotherapeutic work, helping the patient to gain control of symptoms and stabilize eating behaviors.

Patients are often reluctant to consider using medication as part of their treatment, and parents are often reluctant to start an adolescent on a psychotropic medication. These concerns are understandable. The decision to use medication is not a trivial one and should be carefully evaluated. Patients and parents are entitled to a detailed explanation of the pros and cons of a medication trial–a "risk/benefit" analysis. Only if it is clear that medication might substantially benefit the patient and enhance other aspects of treatment should it be considered. This should be true for any prescribed medication, whatever the nature of the illness.

Often patients and families are more concerned about medications used to combat psychiatric illnesses than they are about medications used for medical illnesses. There is often a fear that using medications to assist in the treatment of psychological problems involves some fundamental alteration of the patient's personality or selfhood.

The use of psychiatric medication may be seen as "using drugs to alter one's mental state." In this conception, medication for a psychological problem is viewed as using a chemical to solve a behavioral problem that should be solved by the patient's willpower and understanding—a medical form of drug abuse. Other patients fear that the medication will fundamentally change their experience of themselves, effectively making them into someone not authentically themselves. Still others are concerned that they may become dependent on the medication indefinitely in order to control their eating symptoms.

In fact, there is little to warrant these kinds of concerns. The antidepressants are not drugs of abuse—they do not create a euphoria or "high" and they do not cause psychological dependency or addiction. There is no evidence that they in any way fundamentally alter a person's sense of self. There is also no evidence that these medications produce long-term harm. Early reports that some antidepressants predisposed certain patients to suicidal behavior proved unfounded. Antidepressants are generally intended for use over a limited period of time while the treatment progresses. Ultimately, when eating symptoms have been under control for a reasonable period of time, the medication can usually be gradually tapered and discontinued. For patients with very severe illness characterized by a long and chronic course with severe symptoms, more extended treatment with medication may be necessary.

A variety of antidepressants have been used in the treatment of bulimia and all appear to work equally well. As a result, clinicians usually choose as the first-line treatment an antidepressant that has the most desirable side effect profile, typically one of the medications known as a selective serotonin reuptake inhibitor (SSRI). Prozac is the best-known of this class of antidepressants, but there are now many other equally effective agents available. The SSRIs are generally safe and well tolerated. They are not habit forming, induce no dependency, and do not produce a euphoria or "high." The most common side effects are gastrointestinal, such as upset stomach or diarrhea. In a few cases, these agents may cause patients to feel anxious or "jittery," whereas others may find them sedating. In a minority of patients, these medications may reduce sexual desire and can also interfere with sexual responsiveness. For most patients the side effects are minimal, and many disappear with time.

Eating disordered patients are often particularly concerned about the possibility of medication inducing weight gain. Generally this is not a problem with the SSRIs. In some patients they may cause a small initial weight loss, though this is usually temporary. Weight gain is not a common side effect of these medications. Generally the psychiatrist can minimize side effects by altering the dose or by switching to a different medicine if necessary.

Given all these factors, most clinicians treating patients with severe or persistent bulimic symptoms will recommend a trial of an SSRI. Generally these medications require a week or more to produce beneficial results. Since most clinicians prefer to begin antidepressant treatment at a low dose and raise the dose gradually to a level that is maximally effective, an antidepressant trial often takes four to six weeks. It is important to note that not all patients are helped by these medicines. When a reasonable trial of the medication indicates that it is ineffective, it is discontinued. However, a majority of bulimic patients report that the medication leads to less difficulty in controlling impulses to binge and purge and that it decreases frequency of binge/purge episodes.

For patients with anorexia nervosa, the use of medication is more problematic. For anorexic patients who also have bulimic symptoms, the SSRIs may be useful, although emaciated patients may have physical complications that make the use of the medications more difficult. For anorexic symptoms themselves (restriction of caloric intake, excessive exercise, and preoccupation with food, eating, and weight), medications have generally proven ineffective. This is not for lack of trying. Indeed, over the last decades nearly every medication that seemed remotely likely to be helpful has been tried. Many medications have weight gain as a side effect, so they seemed a logical choice to treat anorexia. Unfortunately none of them produced the desired effect in anorexic patients. Limited research shows that anorexic patients who have regained normal weight may be better able to retain that weight when placed on an SSRI, but these findings are preliminary.

Of course, eating disordered patients may also suffer from other emotional and psychiatric problems in addition to their eating symptoms. These are referred to as comorbid illnesses, meaning that they are distinct illnesses that coexist with the eating disorder. These coexisting disorders may exist as separate disorders, and often they were present before the onset of eating symptoms. In other patients, they may be brought on by the stress of the eating syndrome. For example, a prolonged struggle with eating symptoms may lead to depression. In cases where the comorbid illness precedes the onset of the eating problems, it may worsen as the stress of the eating disorder takes its toll on the patient's energy and endurance. In such cases a psychiatric consultation is particularly important, since it is essential that each problem be identified and specifically addressed in the overall treatment plan.

Common comorbid conditions in eating disordered patients include depression, anxiety or panic disorders, obsessive-compulsive disorders, substance abuse, and personality disorders. Some of the symptoms may be similar to eating disorder symptoms, requiring careful evaluation and detailed exploration of the patient's complaints. For example, typical symptoms of depression include a markedly depressed mood characterized by feeling sad, empty, irritable, or apathetic. Additional depressive symptoms include inability to enjoy oneself, disturbed sleep patterns, decreased energy, agitation, significant weight loss or gain, feelings of worthlessness, decreased ability to concentrate and think clearly, indecisiveness, and suicidal ideation. Clearly some of these symptoms also regularly occur in eating disorders, and it may take a careful psychiatric evaluation to distinguish which symptoms belong to which problem. Like bulimic symptoms, depressive symptoms also often respond to treatment with antidepressants. Where such treatment is indicated, the response to antidepressants may help restore a level of motivation and energy that makes it possible for the patient to make better use of the psychotherapeutic treatment. Clearly, where depression exists along with bulimia, there is an even stronger indication for treatment with an antidepressant, since the medication may help the patient with both conditions.

Similarly anxiety disorders share some symptoms in common with eating disorders. Anxiety disorders are common psychiatric disorders and are typically characterized by consistently excessive anxiety and worry persisting over time, symptoms that are not responsive or minimally responsive to reassurance. Other symptoms include restlessness, difficulty concentrating, sleep disturbance, irritability, and fatigue.

Anxiety disorders may also involve anxiety attacks, which are episodes of intense fear or discomfort with associated symptoms such as pounding heart, sweating, trembling, sensations of shortness of breath, dizziness, and feelings of detachment or unreality. These symptoms are often terrifying and can lead patients to avoid anxiety-provoking situations and constrict their lives in an effort to avoid recurrent panic attacks. Patients in the midst of a panic attack may fear that they are having a heart attack or are otherwise in mortal danger. A number of medications can be useful in the treatment of anxiety disorders. In the past, these disorders were treated with tranquilizers such as Valium, Ativan, or Xanax. Although these medications may be useful in some selected patients, in general we try to avoid them because of the tendency to sedate patients and to induce dependency. Currently a number of newer medications exist that are safe and effective in the treatment of these disorders. These include the SSRI antidepressants discussed above (which are often also effective in controlling anxiety), as well as other medications that are usually first-line treatments for anxiety in eating disordered patients, such as BuSpar. These medications are often useful in controlling anxiety without producing sedation, and they are not addictive. After a period of treatment, the medication usually can be slowly tapered and discontinued.

Obsessive-compulsive disorder is another anxiety disorder that may accompany an eating disorder. Indeed, perhaps one-fifth of anorexic patients have some significant obsessional symptoms. Obsessions are recurrent and persistent thoughts or impulses that are experienced as unpleasant, intrusive, and inappropriate (not ordinary worries about real problems). Compulsions are repetitive behaviors, such as hand washing, checking, counting, or praying, in order to reduce distress or to prevent some imagined dreaded event. Since eating disordered patients are often preoccupied with food and exhibit eating behaviors that appear obsessive, the clinician may wonder whether obsessive-compulsive disorder may be an important aspect of the problem. In fact, among anorexic patients, the one-fifth who have clinically significant obsessive symptoms, have behaviors that go well beyond the usual eating disorder food and weight preoccupations. These obsessive/compulsive symptoms vary greatly but are typically rigidly ritualized behaviors such as counting bites or counting the number of times food is chewed. Other rituals might be cutting food into particular shapes, spitting out food according to some ritualized schedule, or a compulsion to tap fingers or feet a particular number of times before each bite or after each swallow. Medication may help to relieve these symptoms, though generally the medications, even when they reduce obsessive/compulsive symptoms, usually have little or no effect on the patient's nonobsessive anorexic attitudes and behaviors.

These are not the only comorbid symptoms and illnesses for which psychiatric consultation may be useful, but they are the most common. Some patients present more unusual or complex symptom pictures, but the general principles elaborated above still apply. It is important to keep in mind what the psychiatrist can and cannot do. The consulting psychiatrist can provide an expert opinion about the patient's condition from a specialized perspective. The psychiatrist's role does not involve oversight of the therapy as a whole, nor can the psychiatrist offer opinions about the specifics of the therapy itself. When patients have concerns about the effectiveness of the therapy, a second opinion should be sought to evaluate the course of treatment and make recommendations. While this second opinion can be rendered by a psychiatrist experienced in the treatment of eating disorders, other senior professionals can also provide this service.

When meeting with the psychiatrist, the patient should understand that, for the most part, the therapist and psychiatrist will communicate freely, exchanging whatever information is required to make the consultation effective and precise. However, both parties are bound by the same obligation to respect the patient's privacy and to observe confidentiality.

A Family Systems Perspective on Recovery from an Eating Disorder

NANCY THODE

And out of the blue I understood that the family photograph held the answer. That it was really a portrait of a kind of reckless courage, a testament to the great loving carelessness of the heart of every family's life, even ours. That each child represented such risk, such blind daring on its parents' parts–such possibility for anguish and pain–that each one's existence was a kind of miracle.

—*Family Pictures*, Sue Miller

Mary Brown, fourteen years old, 5 feet, 6 inches tall, and weighing 95 pounds, was brought to the Wilkins Center by her mother, Jean. Jean could not understand what had caused Mary's recent refusal to eat and her irritable behavior. According to Jean, Mary had always been an "easy" child, had excelled at school, and had been cooperative at home. Now she was not eating and was having mood swings that upset everyone in the family.

Family therapists think about the development of an eating disorder as a signal that the family is under stress. By stress we mean the emotional and physical reactions we experience as a result of some hurt, loss, pain, anxiety, depression, or sadness that underlie the development of a symptom like an eating disorder. The focus of recovery is the process of understanding the sources of the stress in the family and finding healthy ways to deal with it.

Family therapists focus on stress in the family instead of stress in the individual with the eating problem because they base their interventions on systems theory. Systems theory tells us that all parts of a system are interrelated, that one part of a system cannot be understood without knowing the other parts, and that the whole is greater than the sum of the parts.

A way of conceptualizing the tenets of systems theory is to envision a mobile hanging from the ceiling, all of its pieces interconnected and moving in relation to one another. If we change one piece of the mobile, the whole structure will be thrown out of kilter. To get the mobile back into equilibrium, we would have to remove or add another part or adjust the position of the parts (Richardson 1984). The point is that we cannot know the effect of changing one piece without viewing it as a part of the whole.

A family is another example of a system. In our society we define a family as a system of individuals who have come together through birth and marriage and whose interrelatedness extends backward encompassing all past generations. The behavior, movement, growth, or change in each member affects the behavior of all other members of the family, directly or indirectly. A family is like a mobile, a system of interrelated individuals, each in delicate balance with the others to form a balanced movement of the whole. Feelings or emotions experienced by one family member will affect the feelings and emotions of other family members. Stress experienced by one family member will affect other family members, no matter how carefully we try to keep it to ourselves! Families are emotionally connected.

Focus on the family during the recovery process is not meant to imply that the family is to be blamed for the eating disorder. Blame is not useful or valid in family therapy. Development of an eating disorder is much too complicated a process to blame on any particular factors or people. The factors involved are infinite. What we do know is that if we can change a few of these factors, we can relieve the symptom. This is the piece of reality that is relevant. When a family therapist asks a family member to change a way of behaving or asks a family member to realign a relationship, the request in no way implies blame for the problem. To the contrary, it implies confidence in the ability of that family member to be an agent of change in the family.

To understand and treat an eating disorder, three levels of systems need to be addressed. These are the systems that play a part in symptom development, symptom maintenance, and in recovery:

1. The larger sociocultural system;
2. The family system; and
3. The physiological and emotional systems of the person with the symptom.

Because the sociocultural system and the physiological and emotional systems of the symptomatic family member are addressed elsewhere in this book, I will just briefly define them in the system's context and then return to the subject of this paper, the family.

THE SOCIOCULTURAL SYSTEM

Societies have historically reinforced women's sacrifice of their health in the pursuit of the current ideal of feminine beauty. Examples are the rib-breaking corsets of several generations ago to promote the wasp waist and the practice of binding feet in China (Root, Fallon, and Friedrich 1986). In our present-day society, the current ideal of feminine beauty is to be thin. As a culture we have become obsessed with thinness and issues concerning food, appearance, and body fat, especially for girls and women. Miss America contestants and Playboy Bunnies have gotten progressively thinner in our generation (Garner et al. 1980). Orbach (1982) points out that girls and women receive many conflicting messages about how to get approval, acceptance, and a sense of well-being. But one message is crystal clear–everything will fall into place if a woman is thin. The media gives the message that being thin is not only beautiful but powerful. People flock around thin girls and women. They look self-confident and assured. Thus being thin is equated with power. No wonder studies show that 60 percent of girls have dieted by the age of eighteen (Root, Fallon, and Friedrich 1986). Societal systems are a major influence in the development and maintenance of eating disorders.

THE PHYSIOLOGICAL SYSTEM

For genetic or biochemical reasons, some bodies seem to gravitate toward a higher fat content than others. When people try to diet to a weight below their biologically determined weight in order to conform to the cultural ideal, the physiological response is starvation. The anorexic is in a constant state of starvation. In bulimia, periods of starvation alternate with periods of bingeing and purging. The following gives us an understanding of what happens when people do not eat.

A famous study by Keys, Taylor, and Grande (1950) at the University of Minnesota indicated that when young, healthy, psychologically normal men cut their caloric intake by half for six months and lost 25 percent of their body weight (similar to what takes place in anorexia nervosa), they developed a range of bizarre symptoms: a constant preoccupation with food and difficulty concentrating on anything else; tendencies to hoard food and to spend hours bingeing; problems with depression, irritability, outbursts of anger, anxiety, nervousness, apathy, and low sexual desire; and trouble with alertness, comprehension, and judgment. Physical symptoms included sleeplessness, dizziness, headaches, hypersensitivity to noise and light, reduced strength, poor motor control, edema, and visual disturbances. These symptoms are the same as those seen in clients with eating disorders. Thus this study tells us that many of the symptoms we observe in persons with eating disorders are directly related to the starvation process itself. (For more details of physiological aspects, see the first paper in this book.)

A person develops an eating disorder only when she is experiencing emotional stress or is a conduit for family emotional stress, but once the eating disorder has developed, many of the symptoms are physiologically based in the starvation response. Clearly the physiological and emotional systems of the person with an eating disorder are intertwined. Efforts toward emotional recovery must be preceded or accompanied by recovery of the physiological system.

A further complication is that eating disorders become addictions, psychologically and physiologically. However, unlike addiction to alcohol or other drugs, one cannot stop using the substance. One has to eat. This is one of the reasons that eating disorders are difficult to treat.

THE FAMILY SYSTEM

It is believed that individuals organize into family units to carry out certain necessary tasks, like raising children, nurturing and supporting one another, sharing in household duties, and providing security for one another. To carry out these tasks, a family and its members need order (or predictability) and balance. As with any other system, a family will resist change and in the face of change will gravitate toward reestablishing order and balance. "Order" refers to the family's predictable patterns of behaving and reacting, as well as the traditional roles played by members of that particular family.

This all-important order in the family is achieved by "family rules." Family rules are of two kinds, spoken and covert. Spoken rules might include those concerning interrupting one another when talking, and those concerning bedtime, homework, when to watch television, or whose job it is to take out the garbage. Because these rules are spoken, they can be discussed, even questioned, in some families. The covert rules are understood and agreed on by everyone, but they are not openly acknowledged or discussed and may even be denied. For instance, in some families it is not okay to be angry but it is all right to be depressed. In other families men are not supposed to be afraid, but acting angry is acceptable. In some families arguing is not allowed. In other families arguing is the way family members connect with one another (Richardson 1984). Spoken and unspoken rules tend to be passed down from generation to generation (Kerr and Bowen 1988).

The purpose of rules, spoken or covert, is to control the way people relate to one another and to outsiders. The rules keep order, give a family predictability, and keep everything in balance as long as everyone plays by the same ones (Richardson 1984). In most families the spoken rules are adjusted and changed as the needs of the family and family members evolve during the normal course of the life cycle. The unspoken rules also change, but with more difficulty, since the family is often not consciously aware that they are operating under these particular rules.

All families operate with both kinds of rules. A rule only becomes a problem when it inhibits family members from dealing directly with stress or anxiety. When such a prohibition has been in effect for a number of generations, stress builds up and becomes part of the family heritage, which is passed down from generation to generation much like family heirlooms. Stress buildup is not a direct result of the pain and losses the family encounters over the generations. Rather, it results from the effect of the stressful events on the relationships within the family. And this effect is dependent on the family rules for handling stressful events.

Sources of Stress in the Family

Family therapists work with the family to understand what is stressful and how the family deals with it. I ask families to imagine a stress bucket that sits in the middle of the living room floor. All the stress experienced or inherited by each family member is poured into the bucket. A symptom in the family, such as an eating disorder, is an indication that the bucket has overflowed. The family has developed stress buildup. For the purpose of organizing our thinking we can look at stress as coming from three main sources.

Predictable family life-cycle stress. The first source results from predictable family life-cycle stages (Carter and McGoldrick 1989). These stressors are normal and expected, and result from the family's evolution over time. Therapy with families has shown that certain stages of the family life cycle are particularly stressful: birth of the first child, children in adolescence, and children maturing and going off on their own. This is true partially because of the tremendous changes involved in the ways family members relate to one another as a result of these transitions.

For example, a couple with a new baby may be joyous about the new addition. However, they must also adjust their marital relationship to include a relationship as coparents. In addition, as husband and wife take on parental roles, they find that the relationship with their own parents is changing to include their own roles as parents and their parents' new roles as grandparents. All this change is normal, but it is stressful. There will be a period during which the family mobile is out of kilter as a result of the birth. In time, as new ways of relating to one another are developed, the family mobile will find balance in its altered state and the family can again go about its business.

Unpredictable stress. The second category of stress results from unpredictable events that take place in the family's environment, such as illness, war, or financial setbacks like the loss of a job. This category includes daily tensions like someone being mean to a family member or having a bad day at the office or at school. All these concerns, major and minor, land in the family stress bucket. However, each time a family member copes with stress in a healthy way by changing the situation that caused the stress or by negotiating a settlement with someone who made him or her angry or even by just having a good cry and letting the hurt go, stress is ladled out of the bucket.

Inherited stress. The third source of stress results from painful situations that were not laid to rest in previous generations and are passed down to the next generation. This stress is made up of all the hurts, losses, and angers that have been experienced by previous generations but have not been worked through to an understanding or peaceful resolution.

An extreme example is a family with a history of loss in the Holocaust. I have encountered five anorexic girls during the last several years who have a history of loss through the Holocaust in their grandparents' generation. The grandparents of the eating disordered child suffered the overwhelming pain of losing much of their family of origin to the Holocaust in Europe. They escaped, married, and had children, whom they tried to protect from their overwhelming feelings of loss by not talking about their pain. It is the grandchild who developed anorexia nervosa. It is unlikely that these grandparents would have been able to fully process their grief. Their loss was too overwhelming. Their child, the mother or father of the anorexic patient, who is one generation removed, is better able to work with the grandchild to process the pain, helplessness, anger, and often guilt that has been passed down through the generations. The same need to process hurt or loss exists in families that have a history of abuse, incest, alcoholism, depression, untimely death, or other painful event that has not been fully processed. Although it is not uncommon to encounter a history of extreme tragedy in families of persons with eating disorders, a simple cause-and-effect relationship should not be assumed. Development of an eating disorder is far more complex than that would imply.

As unprocessed emotional issues in one generation are passed to the next, stress builds up. Further, the more anxiety and stress that is passed down in a family, the more vulnerable that family is to added stress from the family life cycle or unexpected events and the more likely that someone in the family will develop a symptom. (Sometimes one can only guess why one family member develops the symptom rather than another. Why the symptom that develops is an eating disorder is often a mystery, although it can be related to the importance the family places on food or appearance.)

Family therapists assume that stress buildup is related to faulty interactions between people. The closer people are to one another emotionally, the greater the possibility of stress buildup in the presence of rigid family rules. Sometimes individuals are unable to deal directly with hurt or anger because of circumstances beyond their control or because family rules prohibit them from working through issues. When the persons directly involved do not deal directly with their hurt or anger, for example, on a one-to-one basis, the pain can be relieved by *triangulating*, that is, bringing in another person or persons. This unconscious and natural process relieves the stress in the original parties but often results in transferring stress onto the third party. This process of triangulating is the way stress is passed down through generations or among family members.

The following is a common example of triangulating: Marge finds herself getting angry at her husband, Fred, who arrives home for dinner later and later. She has difficulty confronting him directly, so she calls her mother and tells her in great detail about what a louse Fred has become. The effect of this call to Mom is to lessen Marge's anger and frustration because she has let off steam. But there are other effects: The issue between Marge and Fred is not dealt with, and Mom finds herself worrying about her daughter's marriage and what, if anything, she should do to help. Thus stress has been transferred from the original twosome to a triangulated party, Marge's mother.

Triangulating is normal. We do it all the time. If we confronted every person who slighted us, we would be exhausted. If the clerk in the market is rude, we might grouse to our best friend and just let it go. It is of concern, however, when we habitually involve a third person to lower tension in a close relationship instead of dealing directly with the issues in the relationship itself.

The example of Marge and Fred is an example of triangulating up the generations. Far more common is the tendency to triangulate down the generations. What follows is an example of how stress was passed down in a family, how it built up, and how it then resulted in the development of a symptom, in this case, an eating disorder. The following case is not meant to explain the cause of eating disorders, as no one really fully knows their cause.

Case Study

John had gotten more and more involved in his work so that he seldom returned home until the kids were ready for bed. Ann, his wife, became increasingly angry and resentful that she was left with the lion's share of the parenting responsibility. She was also hurt by the loss of his companionship. In her family of origin she learned that not only was it not nice to get angry, it wasn't even nice to feel angry. She also learned to "make the best of things," "keep a stiff upper lip," and "don't make waves." (These are examples of covert family rules.) She learned these rules by observing that her parents never dealt directly with each other about dissatisfactions. Ann couldn't even allow herself to have angry feelings, much less express them. Instead of confronting John directly, she became depressed and irritable. John sensed that all was not well with Ann, but he, too, had learned not to ask or "rock the boat" (his family's rule). His solution was to stay at the office even later to avoid the possibility of conflict. The tension continued to build.

One way tension can be resolved without having to confront the scary, painful issues between this couple and thus break the family rules is to focus on something else. If John and Ann can get interested in a third person or object or issue, then tension between them will lessen or at least be put on hold.

Children unconsciously cooperate in this unspoken need because little else is more frightening to them than tension between their parents. Children can distract their parents from the tension in lots of ways: by fighting, getting bad grades, keeping messy rooms, taking drugs or alcohol, and of course by developing an eating disorder.

At the same time that the tension was building between John and Ann, fourteen-year-old Suzy, who was feeling tense and out of control herself, decided to go on a diet. Was she feeling tense because her parents were tense? That may have been part of it. She may also have been feeling tense because she had just moved from junior high school to senior high. She may have been feeling anxious about all the physical changes of puberty, as well as the new social pressures. A host of issues were involved. This was a family that had not learned to deal with stress or anxiety directly, so wherever the stress was coming from it was probable that Suzy would deal with it in an indirect manner.

Eating disorders, as well as other symptoms, are indirect ways of dealing with stress resulting from a difficult or painful experience or unacceptable feelings. Whatever form the diet takes that develops into an eating disorder, it involves an obsession with what to eat and what not to eat. This obsession with food acts like a mask or a smoke screen. It gets Suzy off the track of what is really bothering her. So in one sense it is an effective response to stress and anxiety. It is like "changing the subject."

Not only does it distract Suzy from her own tensions, but the "diet" changes the subject in the family as well. When Suzy stopped eating, Ann and John began to focus on Suzy. They worried, cajoled, got angry, and had long talks about what to do. In the process of concentrating on Suzy the subject was changed, and the tension between the two of them went underground.

In time, however, as Ann and John became more and more focused on Suzy's eating problem, the power struggle between Suzy and her parents became more intense and the three of them became trapped in a circular pattern of reaction to one another from which it became increasingly difficult to escape. Over time, the eating disorder took on the properties of an addiction, so that Suzy became unable to stop. Thus the initial attempt to establish control over her life, as noted earlier, backfired, and she and the whole family were trapped.

TREATMENT

Treating an eating disorder such as Suzy's requires that it be approached from at least two perspectives. One is designed to deal with the symptom itself, the other to deal with the underlying stresses that contribute to the development of the eating disorder in the first place.

TREATING THE SYMPTOM

I often suggest dealing with the symptom by putting the person with the eating disorder in charge of her eating. This does not mean abandoning her to her own devices. It requires that a contract be developed with her and her family outlining what is expected of them, how the contract will be monitored, and what the consequences will be for not living up to the contract. For example, she can resume field hockey once her weight reaches a particular level, or she may go on a trip if she reaches a certain weight by summer. Contracts should also spell out clearly the criteria for hospitalization and how that will be implemented, if necessary. To help the individual take charge, she is given a support network. Key figures are the medical internist, who can provide regular feedback on her progress and state of physical health, and the nutritionist, who can work closely with her on meal plans and, most important, provide her with information and understanding regarding the physiology of starvation and recovery. (The physical process of beginning to eat normally again is difficult because the digestive system and metabolism have gone into slow gear. Papers 1 and 2 of this book deal with these aspects of recovery in greater depth.

When families initially come for treatment, the parents are primarily concerned with managing the day-to-day family life of a child with an eating disorder, that is, managing the symptom. It is frightening to observe a child starving. Parents find themselves going to extraordinary lengths to encourage or force their child to eat.

Tara Smith, for instance, was fifteen when she became anorexic. Mrs. Smith spent hours wracking her brain for foods to buy or cook that would entice Tara to eat. Mr. Smith would bring home the special treats that Tara had always loved, only to have them rejected. In the evening he would drop everything and go to the store because Tara mentioned that some strawberry ice cream might taste good. On his return she had changed her mind. He became furious and berated Tara for being so self-centered. Mrs. Smith had fallen into the habit of cutting Tara's food into tiny bites so it would be easier for her to swallow. She asked the family's cooperation in adjusting their dinner time and menus to suit Tara's schedule. Tara's brother, John, had been told: "Don't argue with Tara. We don't want to upset her. Don't make Tara angry; maybe she won't eat. Don't say or do anything to cause stress to Tara." On the other hand, Mrs. Smith found herself constantly nagging Tara: "Won't you just eat one cracker? What did you have for lunch? Have you eaten breakfast?"

The family's emotional life had become hostage to the eating disorder. Tara's parents were physically and emotionally drained in their efforts to coax Tara to eat. John was angry and felt that the family's attention was revolving around Tara.

Because families often come into therapy describing a situation similar to the Smiths', the family therapist, as the first order of business, will commonly try to help the family step back from issues around eating and let the adolescent take charge. The idea is that once food is no longer the arena of a power struggle in the family, the adolescent will begin to develop her own judgment and make more responsible decisions about food (with the support of her nutritionist and therapist). This, of course, is one goal of therapy— that the adolescent becomes responsible for maintaining the health of her own body, a metaphor, if you will, for developing autonomy.

This process is far more complex than it sounds, but the simplest way to envision it is to imagine the family treating the adolescent as though she were eating normally. Only occasionally buy special foods. Expect her to adjust to the family's meal schedule. Avoid overprotecting her from the emotional life of the family. Perhaps most important, the parents need to reach agreement with each other as to the best ways to approach these changes so that they can present a united front and thus not sabotage each others' efforts (Siegel, Brisman, and Weinshel 1988). The process of family members stepping back from managing the adolescent's eating is a long and difficult one. Each step must be fully explored, planned, and reported in the next session. Did the adolescent eat less or more when Mom stopped cutting her food? How did she feel? How did everyone else respond and feel? If Mom was not able to make the change, what interfered?

The family's retreat from its overinvolvement in the eating disorder symptom must be undertaken with great care. The therapist needs to assist families in developing as complete an understanding as possible as to the effect of change on each family member and the family system. If Mom or Dad stops worrying about what Sue is eating, will Sue feel unloved and abandoned and become more depressed? Will Mom and Dad turn to worries concerning another child? No longer distracted by the eating disorder, will they become aware of strains in their own relationship? Will they come face to face with the often painful tasks demanded by their own life-cycle stage, such as coping with middle age, the death of their own parents, and the realization of their own mortality, retirement, and empty-nest concerns? Focusing on the daily behavior of a sick child can distract family members from a variety of concerns. Before deciding how families should change the way they respond to food issues, I ask the family to explore as fully as possible what might confront them were the focus of concern to change.

TREATING THE UNDERLYING STRESSES

In looking for underlying stresses that contributed to the development of the eating disorder, keep in mind the idea of multicausality.

Let us return to our example of Suzy and her family. The tension between her parents did not cause Suzy's eating disorder. Going to high school did not cause it nor did the fact that Grandmother and Grandfather passed down the family rule: "Don't talk about dissatisfactions—it might cause conflict." Nor was it caused by the societal preoccupation with thinness. However, even though none of these caused the eating disorder, they can all be seen as possible contributing factors.

Having so many factors operating is helpful in treating the eating disorder. We know from systems theory that if one part of a system is changed, the whole system is affected. Thus a change in any one of the factors may have an impact on Suzy's eating disorder.

Parents are one of the most important influences in a child's life, and therefore they often wield the most power to effect change in the family and in the child. This is why parents are asked to take an active role in the treatment and recovery process.

The following is an example of how a family might experience significant change during the course of therapy:

I first saw Mary Brown when she was brought to the Wilkins Center weighing 95 pounds, as described at the beginning of this paper. It was the winter of her first year in high school. Susan, her sister, was a senior and was planning to leave for college the following September. From family life-cycle theory I knew that, consciously or unconsciously, the parents would perceive this event as the first step toward the day when their role as parents would diminish dramatically. Moreover, Mary's maternal grandfather had recently been critically ill. So in addition to facing her diminishing role as a parent, Mary's mother, Jean, was also confronting the inevitability of losing her own parent and was thus being reminded of her own mortality, another normal but stressful life-cycle event. Jean was not currently working outside the home, since she felt she should be home for her children during their teenage years. She had a clear sense of what Mary's behavior should be in areas such as eating, the clothes she wore, friends, and so forth, and devoted considerable energy to seeing that Mary, as well as Susan, followed her rules. In the past she had worked as an interior designer, and she missed that aspect of her life. Mary's father, George, had a demanding job that kept him away from home many evenings.

So far I had not heard anything particularly out of the ordinary about this family. Yes, the family was experiencing a number of life-cycle changes, but so do all families. Talking further, I found that Jean's father was alcoholic. Her mother, though severely obese, managed to be the main support of the family. Jean spent her child-hood worried about her mother's obesity, helping her mother with her younger siblings, and being very careful not to rock the boat by expressing any of her own wants or needs or negative feelings. Mary's father, George, came from a family in which the father had died young of lung cancer attributed to heavy smoking. His mother had been overweight, and this had been a subject of his father's scorn. George worked hard after school and weekends to help sup-port the family. As in Jean's family, he grew up walking on eggshells, careful not to upset the family's tenuous balance.

Susan and Mary had participated in triangles for years, which had kept the lid on the level of stress experienced by the parents. A par-ticularly significant triangle in this family worked in the following way.

Mary's father was distressed that his wife smoked a pack of ciga-rettes a day. Jean wanted to stop but was afraid that if she did she would become obese like her mother. Because smoking had been an important issue in George's family of origin, Jean's habit caused him a lot of anxiety. He could not bring himself to talk to his wife directly about his disapproval, but he and Mary talked about this together. On the one hand, Mary liked these conversations. She did not see her father often and this gave them a connection and a feeling of closeness. On the other hand, she felt uncomfortably disloyal to her mother. As long as George talked to Mary, his anxiety about Jean's smoking was tolerable and the level of tension between the parents was manageable. However, Mary found herself worrying more and more about her mother's smoking. The more Mary pleaded with her mother to stop smoking, the more adamantly Jean expressed her fear of gaining weight.

During the fall of her ninth-grade year, Mary began to diet. Ini-tially this gave Mary a jolt of power. Her parents, especially her father, complimented her on her control. In addition, she was pleasantly surprised to find that her friends at school were impressed with her bone thinness.

As she got thinner and thinner, she lost the ability to concentrate. She fell behind in school, withdrew from friends, was anxious, depressed, irritable, and was even angry and snappy at home, all symptoms of starvation.

These symptoms had a marked effect on the family. Mary's parents became increasingly anxious and frantic about her health and her behavior. Predictably, one result of this anxiety was to take the focus off Jean's smoking problem. In addition, the tension between Jean and George lessened as they came together in a common concern about Mary.

In beginning her treatment Mary met with a nutritionist regularly. All exercise and sports were curtailed, to be reinstated gradually as her weight rose. Individual sessions with Mary were directed to helping her deal with her feelings about eating and body image, as well as focusing on her own areas of concern. The overall focus in family therapy was to uncover the underlying tensions in the family.

Parents who are willing to explore their own sources of tension, either in their current lives or those tensions inherited from their families of origin (and they are usually connected), will greatly enhance the likelihood that their eating disordered child will recover. The work the parents do will have the effect of ladling stress out of the bucket, thereby freeing the whole family to deal with the more manageable issues it encounters during its life cycle.

If in therapy the parents can examine and perhaps modify the family's rules for expressing and dealing with stress, and if they are willing to experiment with airing and negotiating their own hurts and dissatisfactions, several outcomes can be predicted: (1) the tension and anxiety between the parents will diminish, and this in turn will lessen the tension that the child with the eating disorder feels; and (2) the parents, through this experience, will be in a better position to teach their child more constructive ways of dealing with her own anxiety and stress.

Because stress is transmitted through triangulating, I can assume that Mary is in one or more triangles in the family. No triangle can work without the cooperation of all three people. One person may have more power than another, but all are participants. So if one person is enabled to act differently, the triangle will shift and we can work toward having the individuals in each twosome deal with their own issues.

The goal is to get the stress off Mary and back with the original twosome, so the two individuals involved can begin to deal with their own issues. Mary will then be free to deal with the tensions she should be working on, those involved with normal teenage development.

Although the therapist need not involve everyone in a family in the therapeutic process, doing so is clearly desirable and more efficient. Involving everyone does not mean that everyone is in the room each session. Some sessions include the whole family; some may include just the parents; some just the siblings; or some just the family member with the eating disorder. Some sessions include a mix of these groups. The family members with the most strength and flexibility are often those seen the most, since they have the greatest likelihood of effecting change in the family.

As Mary began to gain weight and became a lesser focus of anxiety, the family's attention again turned to Jean's smoking. Several changes occurred to shift the triangle. Mary learned that it was futile to try to control her mother's smoking. She and her father examined the loyalty conflict caused by their discussions regarding Jean, and they agreed to stop talking about Jean's smoking. As Jean began to understand her own family of origin's prohibition against discussing painful feelings and to explore the probable genesis of this rule, she began to see that this might not be a good rule for her family. Mary and her mother began to talk through some of their issues, expressing feelings instead of keeping them hidden.

So Mary and her father gained some distance, and Mary and her mother gained some closeness. The work that Mary's mother did in understanding her own family of origin and the permission given the family to express negative feelings made it possible for the parents to focus on their own issues which, not surprisingly, had more to do with unmet needs in the relationship than with Jean's smoking habit. The communication and negotiations that resulted siphoned off some of the anxiety in their relationship and in turn led to less need to triangulate Mary into their problem. Mary's stress decreased, and she now had more emotional energy to go about the tasks of dealing with her peers and, in general, being a teenager. As the parents began to deal with their own life-cycle changes, they were able to be more reasonable with Mary and give her more age-appropriate responsibilities and freedoms. Experience in renegotiating family roles and rules paved the way for the older child's exit. The family now knew that they could adjust to a change in their relationship with her without losing her. Jean took a full-time job, which she loved, basically getting on with her life. George responded by working fewer hours, getting home for dinner more often, and taking on a more parental role with Mary. Mary's weight stabilized at 115.

OTHER MODES OF FAMILY THERAPY

The above example focused on recovery in a family where the person with the eating disorder was a child and in which the family therapist conducted all therapy sessions: some alone with the child, others with the parents, and still others with the entire family. This is often the most efficient way to work, but occasions arise when it is preferable for another therapist to see the adolescent individually while the family therapist works with the family unit. Using two therapists is best when the adolescent is extremely uncomfortable talking in individual sessions with a therapist who is also seeing her parents. In these cases the individual therapist and the family therapist need to maintain close contact, and all family members need to understand that the two therapists will be working in concert.

Eating disorders often develop in young persons during the family life-cycle stage of "launching." This is why we see such a high incidence of eating disorders among college students. Logistically, it may not be practical for family therapy to be the therapeutic focus for these young adults. The young adult should engage in therapy where she is living or where she is attending school. Parents are strongly urged to seek therapy on their own in order to support her efforts and not to unwittingly sabotage her. Arranging for occasional family sessions during holidays or visits when the family is together is also helpful.

Family therapists often see adults with eating disorders as well. Just as in Mary's case, the focus is on reducing stress in the family. In treating an adult with an eating disorder, the focus is on family-of-origin issues. (Of course, concurrent focus must always be on alleviating the eating disorder symptom.) The person is "coached" to understand the events and rules in her family that led to unresolved stress (Carter and McGoldrick-Orfanidis 1976). She is then encouraged to approach her family of origin in a new manner, one designed to release her from the triangulated position. This work has been shown to be a powerful step toward improving relationships in her adult life. When the person with the eating disorder is married, therapy most often should include the spouse.

The work done by each member of the family of a person with an eating disorder will have a marked effect on the stress level in the family and the tension experienced by each family member. Having learned to approach issues with one another in a direct manner, stress will not build up and the family and each of its members will be free to carry out the primary business of supporting and nurturing one another's growth, development, and security.

References

Carter, B., and M. McGoldrick-Orfanidis. 1976. "Family Therapy with One Person." In P. J. Guerin Jr., ed., *Family Therapy: Theory and Practice*. New York: Gardner.

—, eds. 1989. *The Changing Family Life Cycle: A Framework for Family Therapy*. 2d ed. Boston: Allyn and Bacon.

Garner, D. M., P. E. Garfinkel, D. Schwartz, and M. Thompson. 1980. "Cultural Expectation of Thinness in Women." *Psychological Reports* 47:483–91.

Kerr, M. E., and M. Bowen. 1988. *Family Evaluation*. New York: Norton.

Keys, A., H. L. Taylor, and F. Grande. 1950. *The Biology of Human Starvation*. Minneapolis: University of Minnesota Press. In K. D. Brownell and J. P. Foreyt, eds., *Handbook of Eating Disorders*, p. 307. New York: Basic Books, 1986.

Orbach, S. 1982. *Fat Is a Feminist Issue II*. New York: Berkeley Books.

Richardson, R. W. 1984. *Family Ties That Bind*. Vancouver: Self-Counsel Press.

Root, M.P.P., P. Fallon, and W. N. Friedrich. 1986. *Bulimia: A Systems Approach to Treatment*. New York: Norton.

Siegel, M., J. Brisman, and M. Weinshel. 1988. *Surviving an Eating Disorder: New Perspectives for Families and Friends*. New York: Harper and Row.

5

Relationship to Food as to the World

SUZAN J. RYAN

Food—consuming it, restricting it, hating it, loving it—what does it mean? What is the "food obsession" about for people who suffer from an eating disorder? Their relationship to food can be viewed as a metaphor for how they connect to the world. Linguists have long maintained that one constructs one's world through organizing thought in language. Thus the language in which one frames one's therapeutic interpretations has tremendous importance. The metaphor chosen to connect experiences that the patient knows with experiences that are effectively cut off, unknown to the patient, must be meaningful.

As a therapist, in order to understand my patients, I must immerse myself in the food connection. I must try to grasp the meaning of my patient's fear through food imagery. For example, patients often say that they are afraid of many foods. Labels, they tell me, are inaccurate. Calories and fat content are falsely reported. These patients weigh and measure foods—read and reread labels. Many foods are considered bad no matter what the quantity. These patients do not trust food. It is as though they must be wary at every turn. How, then, can they be expected to enter the process of psychotherapy where they are asked to "swallow" what the doctor says, which is difficult for them. They are very discriminating about what they "take in." Their measuring and weighing of it is how they keep everything on their terms. Anorexics feel that their bodies react to food differently than the bodies of others. They are convinced that if they eat like other people they will "blow up"—be fat. It is the same with the intimacy of therapy. "If I take in what you say, something terrible, over which I have no control, may happen."

Patients who have a binge-purge pattern do not, for the most part, discriminate about what they eat. When they feel hungry, they take in as much as they can. They consume large quantities of food quickly to fill up—to feel okay. Then suddenly, after the frenzy subsides, it is too much. They cannot bear the thought of keeping what they have eaten, so they get rid of it. By doing so, they deny the whole activity. Now it doesn't count. It didn't happen. Whatever they were feeling has gone away. It is flushed down the toilet with the vomit. These patients often appear enthusiastic in their response to the therapist. They seem open and connect quickly. As soon as they cannot tolerate what is being "fed" to them, they reject everything. All the therapist has offered is rejected when anything is unacceptable or too much to contain. It is as though the therapist and patient never discussed certain issues. Such patients say, "I know we talked about it, but as soon as I drove away from your office I forgot the whole thing."

Directly attacking a patient's eating symptoms is often ineffective. Pathological eating behaviors are frequently split off from other more acceptable aspects of the personality structure. Patients with these problems rarely come into treatment voluntarily for the express purpose of changing eating patterns. As a therapist, I want to facilitate the patient's exploration of dynamics. Getting stuck on the literal facts surrounding food may thwart this exploration. Using an eating metaphor, as a working hypothesis, is a way to stay close to the patient and help her gain insight into her destructive behaviors—somehow to integrate the fragmented behaviors that keep her life so tortured.

How can I be helpful to these patients? How can patients understand themselves? Each person's story must be told and retold. Patient and therapist must listen to each part of every story over and over again until the meanings are unmistakable—until the underlying fears are evident and patients are free to live more directly using their own feelings and significant relationships to negotiate conflicts.

The vignettes that follow are a small part of the life stories that patients are trying to understand.

Theresa

Theresa, a young woman in her mid-twenties, entered the office in a terrible mood. She was having great difficulty choosing between two men she found attractive, one man with whom she has had a long-term relationship, and a new man who had entered her life. She wanted to be with the new man without jeopardizing her other relationship. She blurted out, "It is unfair! Why can't I have both? Who makes these rules?" Theresa was bulimic. She binged and purged off and on. She refused to work with a nutritionist. "I can't eat like other people. If I want to go out and consume huge amounts of bread and spaghetti—I will!" Theresa defied everyone. Following the rules was for ordinary people, wimps, people whose lives were like a B movie. Regarding relationships, she was amazed that people don't just do what they want—date two men at once if it meets their needs. She asked: "Doesn't everyone eat what they want and then do something about it or gain weight?"

When Theresa first came into treatment she was bingeing and purging at least once daily and frequently two or three times a day. She was emaciated and exhausted. She felt driven all the time either to take in food or get rid of it. Some of her bingeing was blatant, and she didn't care who saw her eat huge amounts. At other times she would hide her destructive behaviors. Theresa was always tense and frequently angry. It was as though the fight she was having with food extended to everyone. We talked frequently about how she consumed people almost indiscriminately. She would take in everything she wanted just like food and when she was too full, nause-ated, she would throw it up. She defended this as though she had no alternative. "It's the pressure." She would take little responsibil-ity. "It's the food that's around." "If my parents hadn't overindulged me as a child, if they had helped me with limits, I wouldn't have these problems today."

Theresa used her parents, straining the limits of their indulgence and then treating them with disdain. "Why are they so stupid? Don't they know this isn't good for me?" The same theme was reflected in Theresa's relationships with men. She had wanted them to be there for her "on demand," go where she wanted, do what she wanted. She refused to go out of her way for her mother and father, such as to attend any required family functions with them, and yet she had been enraged at them for allowing her to run the show.

Theresa designed her own world, manipulating everyone as though they were props on a stage; when she was all finished, just as when she had binged and purged, she would feel disgusting, empty, and alone. Theresa's task was to connect to others in a way that respected their individuality and needs as well as her own. It was the same with the food—her use of it had to become respect-ful and suited to what was appropriate for Theresa.

When confronted about her disturbed eating patterns, Theresa was unable to gain insight. She felt that her hunger and the need to purge were unique and that no one, surely not the therapist, could understand them. However, when Theresa's interpersonal style was explored, she found it difficult to close the therapist out. Her behav-ior, vis-à-vis her family and men, could not be as easily split off from her self-concept as was her binge/purge cycle. So this was where the therapist entered. We established how it appeared that she used those close to her, like objects for her own pleasure, but she was never satisfied. When she did not respect others and ordered her own needs, she found no true satisfaction. Theresa acted out her "me first" theme in the transference. Her style was incredibly provocative. Whenever I would set a limit for her, or push her in any-way, she would devalue me. These attacks were primitive. I had to stand firm and tell her that she could "get rid" of what I said if she wanted to but that I wasn't going to go away. My recommendations had value and should not be dismissed. More than once during treatment, Theresa wanted to see another therapist. This would be someone working with her family, for example, or someone treating her during a hospitalization. She would schedule a consultation but, like so many of her binges, these initial infatuations or relational binges would turn sour when these therapists challenged Theresa's actions or said she would have to terminate with me appropriately. Seeing these interpersonal behaviors as metaphorically connected to bingeing and purging led to some powerful integrated insights for Theresa. She was able to stay in treatment and work through many of her issues.

Mary

Mary is a quiet, conforming twenty-four year old, who does everything well. She is hard-working and an extreme perfectionist. At work, Mary does a marvelous job. She is conscientious and competent. She overcommits herself and always must do the most work.

Yet she feels a strange uneasiness. If someone else stays late, she must stay later. "It's as if I must do more or I won't be accepted. I can never relax because I may be criticized."

Mary came to therapy five years ago very underweight, frightened, and unable to make decisions. Initially she was rigid, angry, and frightened. She had gained few social skills in high school and was trapped by her need to please family members, especially her mother. Mary was unable to make a purchase without her mother's approval. Very gradually she began to find herself, to have opinions of her own. It was only then that she could relax her incredible food restriction. She began to understand that she could have an opinion of her own without jeopardizing her relationship with her mother. Before the age of twenty, Mary never expressed an opinion contrary to that of her parents. Her only defiance was acted out in a refusal to eat food. She was hospitalized twice for low weight, each time steadfastly refusing psychiatric hospitalization. She has since gone to college and graduate school, moved away from her parents, and taken a job.

At one point late in her treatment, Mary came to our session upset about a skiing experience with her long-standing boyfriend. She had had trouble mastering the beginning elements of downhill.

She fell, was unable to stop herself, and so on. She became so distressed by her apparent lack of skill that she could hardly eat anything for lunch at the lodge. She mistakenly assumed that her poor performance was a result of being overweight and in poor physical condition. (She had, by then, actually settled in at about 110 pounds and is 5 feet, 4.5 inches.)

She was so enraged that she had not demonstrated superior skill during her first try at skiing that she retreated to a safe posture—that of food restriction and weight obsession. She thought: "If I am empty, controlling, I feel more comfortable. Starving helps regain a sense of self. Control over food is the ultimate mastery. If I can keep my body at an incredibly low weight, I must be competent. If I am perfect at nothing else, I will be perfect at this. I will be the thinnest." Although Mary had made progress in treatment, she had difficulty letting down her guard in a crowd. What for everyone else was a recreational experience became a test for Mary.

Mary has talked often in treatment about how her food restriction creates a false sense of security, how it really doesn't mean that she's acceptable or okay. It only means that she is thin. Being able to ski would be just that—not an indication that Mary is good or better or acceptable. Mary must search within herself for healthier ways to be reassured. When Mary needs others most (at times of stress), she restricts her intake, thus effectively setting herself apart. Mary's goal in treatment is to work toward a stronger connection with others so she doesn't have to depend on "food rituals" to get her through tough times. The ideal response to her ski experience, Mary knows, would be a social one. A solution that assumed commonality and interdependence among friends or an understanding bond with her boyfriend would have been more adaptive—in the same way eating a warm nourishing lunch would have been an appropriate response to a tiring cold morning on the slopes.

Elizabeth

Elizabeth, a forty-eight-year-old woman, 5 feet, 5 inches, struggling to keep her weight at 110 pounds, stares at the woman in the cafeteria of a large corporation where she is employed. "They all eat sandwiches, rolls, cake, and so forth, and are not fat! How can this be?" she says to herself. "I know if I eat like that, I will be fat."

Elizabeth remembers, as a child, standing outside the schoolyard and looking in-something terrible would happen to her if she acted "like the other children." Her mother insisted she would be hurt. Her mother told her over and over again that she was incapable of doing anything properly. After the birth of her own two sons, Elizabeth was not permitted to care for them. Her mother fed, bathed, dressed, and cared for them entirely. Elizabeth's husband was "put down" and ignored. He was required to eat his evening meal in a separate room from the family. Contradictions from him would set Elizabeth's mother off, who, in turn, would verbally attack Elizabeth. Elizabeth was sent to work every day and, when she returned home, was to do as her mother said or be threatened with abandonment. Elizabeth never challenged her mother's tyrannical behavior. She feared saying anything that would provoke her mother and cause her to leave. Elizabeth was sure she could not manage alone with her husband and children.

At work, Elizabeth felt like an entirely different person. She worked to please everyone and received recognition for her responsible and perfectionist's exercise of duties. Although the workplace was a safe haven from her mother's fury, Elizabeth needed more control. She began restricting food intake dramatically in her early twenties. She maintained a weight far below what was healthy. She used laxatives to purge herself and feel clean, and practiced rigid food rituals. For example, Elizabeth was unable for many years to eat a sandwich. She had never tasted foods like corn on the cob and watermelon. She reports hearing that these foods were fattening and has therefore completely avoided them. She has been in treatment with me for two and a half years specifically to address the eating disorder. Her earlier treatment focused primarily on her relationship with her mother. She felt more able to work on this problem since her mother's death three and a half years ago.

Now Elizabeth is working on incorporating normal eating patterns into her life, being like others, entering the playground. Elizabeth is reassured in her psychotherapy and nutritional counseling that eating normally will not bring about dire results, that she will not somehow become obese, that, in fact, she is like "other people." Elizabeth needs also to ingest the feelings of those around her. She restricted intimate relationships as she did her food. She would not sit down to supper with her family and, after cleaning the kitchen, would quickly put on her night clothes and retreat to her room. She said, "To get away from the food," but effectively it was to get away from everyone in her family. Once she recognized that her food fears and rituals served to keep her from relating to others, she made dramatic strides in overcoming her anorexia. She found, as she began to eat normally, that she was also able to express her true ideas and feelings and that her family and friends did not leave her as she had feared.

Elizabeth's continual task in treatment is to identify and respond to both bodily and emotional needs.

Sarah

Sarah, a restricting bulimic, has fruit and diet soda from 6:00 A.M. until about 4:00 P.M. Then she has crackers and cheese. She "can't believe" she ate that junk. "I have no self-control. My stomach sticks out. I feel gross." She walks for two or three miles even though the temperature outside is about 25 degrees. She returns home and forces herself to eat a baked potato and a few vegetables. She is restless and agitated. Finally, at 12:00 P.M. she goes to sleep. At 3:00 A.M. she awakes, unable to ward off feelings of anxiety. She gets up and begins baking cookies for her nursery school class. She eats small pinches of raw dough and further castigates herself. She rises in the morning tired, tortured, almost unable to go through another day. She calls a friend and offers to take her children to a movie or ice skating. The friend says, "Why don't you come for dinner after taking the kids out?" She refuses, saying that she has paperwork to do.

Sarah, thirty-six years old, has been coming to therapy for three years. Her life began to fall apart after she lost a private-school job with a built-in social life. Sarah has lived her whole life like a college student. She has never changed the address on her driver's license, which was that of her parents' home. She is always "hanging out," available to work on a project or to baby-sit for a friend. Nothing defines her. It is as though she doesn't stand for anything.

Sarah never feeds herself well. She never eats a normal meal and almost completely avoids any situations in which social eating is required. She takes care of others constantly. She buys them gifts and does them favors. She never lets them care for her or nurture her. She is most comfortable with young children who accept her giving to them and require no mature intimacy. They show her simple affection and never question the fact that she is always the giving one. She gravitates toward impersonal, casual gatherings or activities for which it doesn't matter whether she shows up. These kinds of relationships protect Sarah from having to receive favors—metaphorically, to be fed by anyone.

Sarah's eating pattern is chaotic, with the exception of some health-store-type laxative cereals and fruit. She eats nothing that doesn't produce guilt. She often walks around her village looking into the pizza parlor, local restaurant, or yogurt shop yearning to satisfy herself but unable to do so. She fears someone may see her and what would they think? So she walks home drinking a carry-out diet soda, eating the crackers she keeps in the trunk of her car. This empty chaotic eating pattern parallels her relationships. She has many acquaintances. People think of her as a pleasant, responsible person. When she allows herself superficial, social contact, she never shares a meal, literally or symbolically. No one knows the "meat" of her issues with life. She confides her dreams or her fears to no one. She has never felt intimate with anyone. If Sarah does eat a normal meal, she must purge. If on occasion she has a drink and shares her feelings with a friend, she worries excessively that she has said "too much." She often avoids the friend for weeks, undoing, or purging as it were, the intimacy.

She was not close to anyone as a child, with the exception of one sibling whom she felt she had to protect. As Sarah's despair grew, so did her sense of uselessness and her emotional isolation. Thus Sarah's interior life is mirrored in her inability to feed herself appropriately or be fed in a social situation. We talk often about how she feels hollow and lonely but is unable to risk "taking in" a normal meal or persons and holding on to it or them long enough for digestion or connection to occur.

In psychotherapy Sarah looks at what has become of her friendships over the years. If she can be someone's backup to cover a community event, baby-sit, bake a cake, and so forth—all is well. Once she cannot maintain this hit-or-miss relationship, she backs away. Adult friends share thoughts, share time; they commit something of themselves to each other. Unfortunately this kind of relating is as foreign to Sarah as is the idea of enjoying a complete dinner. So I work literally and metaphorically at helping her to sample better and better appetizers.

Kathryn

Kathryn is beautiful, very bright, and doing well professionally after obtaining a graduate degree. She works out at a gym and has a healthy-looking body. Kathryn has been in treatment for four years for bulimia. Her pattern of interacting parallels her food behavior. When Kathryn meets a young man, within a matter of days, sometimes hours, she finds herself swept up by him. He is seen as "perfect" for her—the kind of person she's been looking for. She is unable to look at differences, potential problems, or interactional patterns. When questioned, she has little insight. Everything is perfect. This relationship is "it." It is going to change her life. Quickly she becomes possessive. She plans her life around him. When she begins to feel closed in, she may speak with an old boyfriend or even have a fling with another man. She lies about her contact or indiscretion. She manipulates situations to hide what is going on and always justifies her behavior, blaming her situation on the way the men treat her. When the relationships become chaotic—which they always do—and finally end, Kathryn paints a picture of the man as a totally insensitive person. It is never she who acted inappropriately.

With food, Kathryn acts similarly. She has had a pattern of bingeing and purging for more than eight years. She refuses to look at her eating patterns. She won't see a nutritionist or keep regular food records. She won't look at her behavior. She insists that forces outside herself cause the eating problems. She avoids taking responsibility for her binges by stealing her binge food. Healthy, acceptable food is bought and paid for—binge food is stuffed into oversized pocketbooks. This behavior is totally inconsistent with the patient's value system, yet she persists because the behavior permits her to continue irresponsible eating without acknowledging it beforehand. Then she undoes her binge by purging—she doesn't pay, neither in reality nor symbolically, for the binge food.

Kathryn had been going from one short-term work position to another, gaining recognition—everyone loved her—everyone thought she was doing a good job. She made sure she moved around a great deal and that no supervisor was regularly looking over her; she hated being totally accountable. Like an addict, she needed to manipulate her environment so she could slip away to binge and purge when so compelled. She was a master at creating plausible excuses. She knew she was cheating those she served. She knew, regardless of the rave reviews, that her performance was far below her abilities.

Kathryn's bulimia led her to betray her value system in several arenas. Kathryn manipulated the environment so she could be free to binge, but in reality she was a slave to her compulsion—never free—always trapped by her need to create space for destructive behavior. The dance of denial that she does with food is reflected in her professional life and her personal relationships. When someone comments on how beautiful she is and what a great body she has, she feels like a fake because of how she abuses her body. Recognition at work rings a hollow note in Kathryn's conscience. When friends console her about these ex-boyfriends—saying they were "no good" or "screwed up"—Kathryn never looks at the total relationship. In every arena Kathryn ends up with the sensation of one who has just purged. She feels empty, guilty, alone—she has no plan for the next time. She feels her compulsions will override her judgment. She will binge on another man, a vulnerable supervisor, ice cream, and cookies—purge and then feel empty.

These vignettes are only a tiny piece of each patient's life, yet they embody an important element in each person's pain. The eating disorder reflects, in metaphoric terms, the troubled themes of these women's daily existence. The goal of our work is to reduce the need for metaphor, by first becoming immersed in the metaphor and then moving the patient to talk out feelings rather than managing them through ritualized and destructive behaviors.

When we listen carefully to a story or a melody over and over again, we touch on meanings that are at first glance hidden. So it is with the stories our patients tell. At first we hear only their prose: how they feel, how they act, and how they understand their food obsessions. Later, these stories transform into ever changing poetry with many meanings. Marcel Proust wrote: "The real voyage of discovery consists not in seeking new landscapes but in having new eyes." Recovery is nothing other than a healing voyage of discovery.

6

The Therapeutic Use of Humor in the Treatment of Eating Disorders; or, There Is Life Even with Fat Thighs

SARITA BRODEN

"What is *real*?" asked the Rabbit one day, when they were lying side by side near the nursery fender, before Nana came to tidy the room. "Does it mean having things that buzz inside you and a stick-out handle?"

"Real isn't how you are made," said the Skin Horse. "It's a thing that happens to you. When a child loves you for a long, long time, not just to play with, but *really* loves you, then you become Real."

"Does it hurt?" asked the Rabbit.

"Sometimes," said the Skin Horse, for he was always truthful. "When you are Real you don't mind being hurt."

"Does it happen all at once, like being wound up," he asked, "or bit by bit?"

"It doesn't happen all at once," said the Skin Horse. "You become. It takes a long time. That's why it doesn't often happen to people who break easily or have sharp edges or who have to be carefully kept. Generally, by the time you are Real, most of your hair has been loved off, and your eyes drop out, and you get loose in the joints and very shabby. But these things don't matter at all, because once you are Real you can't be ugly, except to people who don't understand."

"I suppose *you* are Real?" said the Rabbit. And then he wished he had not said it, for he thought the Skin Horse might be sensitive. But the Skin Horse only smiled.

"The Boy's Uncle made me Real," he said. "That was a great many years ago; but once you are Real you can't become unreal again. It lasts for always."

Margery Williams's wonderful, poignant, and ever timely Velveteen Rabbit about the rabbit in search of himself and his role in life could be the perfect paradigm for sufferers of anorexia nervosa, as well as sufferers of bulimia. These are people with "sharp edges" who "break easily," who feel ugly and unwanted. But most of all they feel misunderstood and unloved. They are reluctant to become real, for they fear that the world around them will see them as unattractive and unworthy of love. They therefore bury their needs and longings under the obsessive/compulsive mantle of an eating disorder and retreat into an unreal world made up of calories, numbers on a scale, and portion sizes, shutting out a world they perceive as threatening and dangerous. This is a world that has made them feel worthwhile only if they look a certain way, act a certain way, or behave in a certain way, a world that generally finds them acceptable only if they are "unreal."

In my work with eating disordered clients, I have seen that some of the key issues for a successful therapeutic relationship are empathic listening, an understanding of the person behind the disorder, a sound theoretical base, an ability to make the client feel understood, and, just as important, a good sense of humor. Psychotherapy, by its very nature, is characterized by an intense joint effort by therapist and client to delve into and comprehend the needs, feelings, fantasies, realities, and fears of the client. This intense relationship requires many tools on the therapist's part: Humor is probably one of the most potent in the therapist's arsenal (Rosenheim and Gabriel 1986).

Amy, an extremely bright, accomplished seventeen-year-old student, had been in therapy with me for almost a year and a half. She was at the top of her class academically, was one of the best athletes in her high school, and had just been accepted to one of the best colleges in the country. She had been suffering from anorexia since the age of fourteen, and, although she had made progress in her weight gain and had developed insight into the genesis of the disorder, she was still struggling with self-esteem. Each newly acquired pound detracted from her self-image. She had enormously high expectations for herself and was rigid about her performance, berating herself mercilessly if she did not reach her self-imposed goals and punishing herself physically by starving, stating repeatedly, "If I can't be the best at whatever I set myself to do, I'll at least be perfect in my diet. I'll keep my thin thighs and be the best runner on my team." Cognitive and psychodynamic interventions addressing these distortions in her thinking had little or no effect.

At one particular appointment, she came in and happily showed me a watch she had acquired over the weekend. The queen of hearts made up the face of the watch, and she was particularly pleased to have found it because she already owned watches with the king and the jack. As she talked she complained that as excited as she was to have found it, she was troubled because it did not keep time accurately:

AMY: It bothers me that it runs slow. Of the three face cards, this was the one I wanted the most.

THERAPIST: Do you know why the queen runs slow?

By now Amy was used to my bantering and joking in our sessions. She was a very serious youngster, who nevertheless appreciated my humor and storytelling and had loosened up enough to tell humorous stories herself from time to time. She had stated at one point in the therapy that she felt I had helped her because I was "real," as opposed to other adults in her life who talked down to her, patronized her, acted "fake." Amy herself felt "fake." Most of her adolescent life had been spent creating a persona that pleased other people, and she was thoroughly and sincerely perplexed as to who the "real Amy" was. Therefore, when I asked her about the watch's timekeeping abilities, a slow smile of anticipation spread across her face.

AMY: Tell me, why does the queen run slow?

THERAPIST: It's probably because underneath all those heavy skirts, she has fat thighs. But isn't it amazing, Amy? She's *still the queen!*

Amy burst into laughter. My absurd comment showed her, with more clarity than any previous interpretation, that her obsessive striving for the "perfect/thin body" that would exemplify her "success" in life had stopped her from becoming a "real" person. She understood my message, that a person might not reach a particular goal and could still like herself (regardless of body shape) or that a person might find a way to reach the pinnacle without incurring the "sharp edges" of an emaciated body.

In the literature, many authors, belonging to different schools of therapy, have apparently recognized the potential for humor in psychotherapy. Among its major benefits are alleviating anxiety and tension; overcoming exaggerated seriousness; creating an atmosphere of closeness and equality; providing an acceptable outlet (by the client) for feelings of hostility and anger; fostering the capacity for self-observation; enabling emotional catharsis (Rosenheim 1977); promoting intimacy, humanness, and a more informal working alliance; and, of course, providing a wonderful and safe means of communication. In the case of eating disordered clients, we can add to the therapist's resources the use of levity, which shows we are not afraid to poke fun at ourselves, as well as at clients' own myths and distortions. We also offer a role model to aid in loosening some of their rigid control and perfectionism (Roncoli 1974). The joke, pun, anecdote, or appropriate story can be a teaching instrument of unique efficacy (Rosten 1968).

A prerequisite for the use of levity in therapy is the therapist's comfort with humor. My predilection is for puns and word play, and on numerous occasions I have used these with some success.

Lisa

Lisa had been referred to me with a diagnosis of bulimarexia. She was twenty-seven years old, the oldest of three children, and essentially the family's caretaker. Her mother was a severely depressed woman with a history of multiple psychiatric hospitalizations, and her father was an emotionally distant man who had been an alcoholic for most of Lisa's life. Lisa cared for her siblings, tended to her mother, and enabled her father to continue functioning by assuming most of the family's responsibilities. She was the proverbial good girl—always there for everyone, feeling totally empty as far as any personal satisfaction was concerned but convinced that she did not deserve any more than what she had. She had begun a serious diet at age twenty-two in an effort to find something that would give her a sense of control and a measure of satisfaction. The diet had rapidly progressed to starvation alternating with episodes of bingeing and purging. She felt proud and "good" on the days she starved but never failed to berate herself for the binge/purge episodes, which she perceived as one more indication of her global worthlessness and failure.

Lisa was a secondary school teacher and an avid reader and lover of music but was extraordinarily serious and devoid of a sense of humor. She could talk about her life in intellectual terms but was unable to tap into any of her feelings. Any attempt to make an interpretation addressing her feelings elicited a stony look and a denial followed by silence. It was obvious that allowing herself to feel was a mine field she was not ready to cross.

She had been seeing me for almost six months when she started a particular session by telling me a dream she had had the night before. Lisa was quite concrete and had let me know in many ways that she preferred to talk about her starving, exercising, and binge/purge episodes rather than any possible reasons why she might be engaging in the behavior. I was therefore quite surprised when she began telling me about a dream that had so disturbed her that she remembered it clearly upon awakening: She had felt (in the dream) a terrible itching on her scalp that was "driving her crazy." When she went to scratch herself, she found to her horror and disgust that her head was full of crawling lice. "It was horrible," she continued, "no matter how much I scratched, the lice were still there."

"I guess your dream is telling you that you have been feeling pretty lousy," was my immediate retort.

Her mouth opened in surprise at my statement, and a smile spread slowly across her face. It was the first genuine response I had seen, and it was followed shortly by the first tears she had ever shed in the course of her treatment with me.

The pun, which targeted her repressed feelings and addressed with immediacy and poignancy how unhappy she was, had had more impact than any other interpretation up to this point. It had been a nonthreatening response to her distress, and with the smile and the tears she told me that she was ready to alter her narrow perceptions of her symptom. I felt, for the first time since she started seeing me, that she had really connected to me and was ready to trust me. No small feat for a person who had learned to distrust, and with good reason, most people in her life.

According to Driscoll (1978), the use of appropriate humor is one way to make material more acceptable. Humor can break the tension when things get too serious, and the amusement and enjoyment are a welcome alternative to the uneasiness or pain patients too often experience. In a lighter atmosphere, patients may come to see their concerns as more tolerable, and the toughest material can be better managed. Laughter can go a long way toward easing anguish. By accepting or even enjoying the material in the sessions, patients begin to accept themselves better and begin to improve their outlook on life. Patients who laugh in their sessions tend to reveal information more readily, making our job of assessment easier and speeding the therapeutic process. From the first session, be it individual or group, I attempt to put the patient at ease by acknowledging her difficulty in being there and having to share her difficulties and unhappiness with a stranger. If appropriate, I will use humorous banter to make patients feel more at ease and to make the experience less formal, less threatening. At times, of course, humor is totally inappropriate: If a person is severely depressed or has experienced a loss or tragedy in her life, forced humor would not only be absurd, it would certainly backfire.

Humor, like many other process-oriented interventions in treatment, should be used in an appropriate and balanced way. As mentioned above, humor is a wonderful tool that necessitates not only a therapist who is comfortable with its uses but also a person who is aware of its parameters and risks. Many authors have questioned the wisdom of using humor in the context of psychotherapy, warning about its possible pitfalls. In 1905 Freud wrote that humor "has in it a liberating element . . . it is something fine and elevating . . . what is fine about it is the triumph of narcissism, the ego's victorious assertion of its own vulnerability" (Freud [1905] 1926). But he also spoke to the possibility that humor was a reflection of underlying anxiety, bitterness, or unspoken hostility (Freud [1905] 1960). Many other authors have questioned the use of humor in therapy. Greenson (1977) pointed out that patients can cover hostility and anger with humor and sarcasm. Paul (1978) agrees that a patient's humor or teasing is often disguised hostility, and Kubie (1971) is adamant in stating that a therapist's use of humor might stem from aggressive, hostile feelings toward the patient. He adds that, for a beginning therapist, using humor could divert the patient's stream of feeling and thought from spontaneous channels, act as a defense against the therapist's anxieties, lead to doubt about the therapist's seriousness, and distort transference phenomena.

If humor or jokes are excessively or inappropriately used, the patient may begin to doubt if he or she is being taken seriously. Both patient and therapist may, if not watched carefully, resort to the use of humor to avoid dealing with difficult, conflicted, or painful areas and thereby inhibit the therapeutic process (Haig 1986).

However, when the therapist is comfortable with his or her ability to use humor appropriately, when the same sensitivity that we expect a therapist to exhibit in other areas of the treatment process is applied to the use of humor, it can indeed be an invaluable tool, especially when working with an adolescent population.

My adolescent/young adult group has been meeting regularly and faithfully for about nine months. With the exception of one person who left because she had to be hospitalized, the membership has been steady. The girls seem to like one another; some have developed a support network outside the group; and most of them are able to relate to one another in the here and now. The group was cohesive and functioning well—but it was much too serious! My occasional attempts at puns and humor (i.e., "I guess you can't have your cake and eat it, too"; "That statement really gives us food for thought"; "Tell us again about swallowing your anger or being starved for attention") were met with smiles or a polite chuckle at best—until the time Karen, an outgoing, verbal sixteen year old who had been flirting with several forms of bulimia, told the group about the previous night's experience. She related that her mother, on the pretext of "helping her straighten out her closet," had found several of the empty or near-empty boxes of laxatives Karen had been using on and off for several weeks.

"Wow! You should have seen her!" she said. "If you guys thought she used to get angry at me before, that was nothing! This time the shit really hit the fan!"

The laughter that ensued, spontaneous and honest, was a catalyst for the group and the group process. Karen's unplanned joke/pun helped her understand, probably better than a "formal/serious" interpretation, the tremendously hostile components of her bulimic behavior.

In conclusion, humor can be a powerful and important tool in psychotherapy if used appropriately and with sensitivity. Adolescents especially have trouble participating in the therapeutic process if they perceive the therapist as patronizing and "fake." Humorous interventions and banter are a way of lessening their discomfort and making them feel they are being treated as equals.

Humor is, of course, inexorably linked to the therapist's personality and to his or her degree of comfort with its usage; but when used by a skilled practitioner, it can help patients gain an objective view of their behavior, point out the self-damaging effects of black-and-white thinking, debunk some of their myths and distortions, and, most of all, cement the therapeutic alliance.

References

Driscoll, Richard. 1978. "Humor in Pragmatic Psychotherapy." *Handbook of Humor and Psychotherapy*. Professional Resource Exchange, 133.

Freud, S. [1905] 1926. "Humor." *International Journal of Psychoanalysis* 9:16.

———. [1905] 1960. *Jokes and Their Relation to the Unconscious*. Translated by J. Strachey. New York: Norton.

Greenson, R. 1977. *Technique and Practice of Psychoanalysis*. New York: International University Press.

Haig, Robin A. 1986. "Therapeutic Uses of Humor." *American Journal of Psychotherapy* 40, no. 4 (October): 549.

Kubie, L. 1971. "The Destructive Potential of Humor in Psychotherapy." *American Journal of Psychiatry* 128:861–66.

Paul, I. 1978. *The Form and Technique of Psychotherapy*. Chicago: University of Chicago Press.

Roncoli, M. 1974. "Bantering: A Therapeutic Strategy with Obsessional Patients." *Perspectives in Psychiatric Care* 12:171–75.

Rosenheim, Eliyahu. 1977. "Humor in Psychotherapy: An Interactive Experience." *American Journal of Psychiatry* 18:548–91.

Rosenheim, Eliyahu, and Golan Gabriel. 1986. "Patient's Reactions to Humorous Interventions in Psychotherapy." *American Journal of Psychotherapy* 40, no. 1 (January): 111.

Rosten, L. 1968. *The Joys of Yiddish*. New York: McGraw-Hill.

7

Jodie's Story

DEBRA BADER

In his essay, "Grimm's Greatest Tale," Stephen Jay Gould (1991) said, "We must never doubt the power of names as Rumpelstiltskin learned to his sorrow." So it is with anorexia nervosa and bulimia. In the past brief time span leading up to this paper, I have had occasion to address audiences of schoolteachers, schoolchildren, parents, alcoholism counselors, and therapists who all seem inclined to define these symptoms as a disease entity and to launch a battle against it. I fear becoming a spinner of the tale by citing data that are true and factual without looking at how an individual uses the world around her. For example, the cultural pressure for thinness colludes with women who are eating disordered. True, but that offers an incomplete explanation. Certainly our culture offers a language that lends itself to individual creativity. I am thinking of the "bulimic-like" headline in the *New York Times* review of the film *Regarding Henry*—"The Treasures of the 80's Turn to Junk in the 90's." The capacity to make use of the cultural language as a focus for dysphoric affect is itself an attempted mastery (Krueger 1988).

The spectrum of character development in which we find these symptoms is broad. Eating disturbances are symptom pictures existing on a continuum from the food-restricting anorexic at one extreme to the binge eater at the other, either normal or overweight. The symptoms vary in cause and function (Ceasar 1988; Gesensway 1988).

Paul Hamburg (1989) says that a symptom is a sign that suggests a mystery. "We should be intrigued by the multiple clues it suggests to us, themes of orality, anality, consumption, the body ego, control, desire, humiliation, and so forth. The richness of these themes is striking. Depending on our theoretical bias, we might privilege one theme or another and search for the single, best, all-encompassing interpretation of the symptom-sign." Hamburg suggests that we not obscure the layerings of meanings with our own need for explanation and certainty.

Often the symptom is all a person has, her only way of communicating. While forming an alliance with the architect of this complex construction, one is always mindful of the serious physical consequences of anorexia and bulimia. Therefore the diagnostic workup will include consultation with an internist to determine the need for further tests or hospitalization. Then the therapist can proceed with a range of possible treatment interventions that grow out of an analytic understanding of that patient, including whether to focus on symptoms. Nutritional counseling and group therapy may be appropriate on consideration of the whole problem.

Whenever I am invited to speak about eating disorders, I always want to ask "Whose?"—for each is specific to the individual. For the following account of Jodie's symptom-signs and their relation to what they signify, I am indebted to the theoretical work of Paul Hamburg (1989), whose work derives in part from the theory of deconstruction as put forth in the 1970s by Jacques Derrida (1978; described in Hamburg 1989, 133). Interpolating this theory, originally applied to literary and philosophical criticism, into therapeutic work, Hamburg illustrates the creative usefulness of searching out the many-layered meanings of a symptom by metaphorical and associative ways of thinking. As he does, I "play" with this material and have left space for the reader to do so as well. Insert yourself into the spaces and ambiguities, and uncover unexpected latent possibilities.

Jodie must have been a beautiful baby—round and fair—who made bubbles of sound. Early in treatment, she related a dream about a baby: "There was a bubble that one could inject with sperm and a baby would grow in it. I injected the bubble and saw two masses in it separate, one was kidneys and one was a baby. Then I had to go and get gas at Dunkin' Donuts. My mother held the bubble. There were lots of waiters and waitresses. I came back and the baby was born. It was big with lots of thick, short hair and looked like me. I held it and it touched my hair and said, 'You have such pretty hair.' "

"What do you make of this?" I asked.

"I want to be admired," she said.

Jodie was going to be her own baby and I was to wait, the patient onlooker. She would take nothing from me. And she talked to me in the baby language of the body ego.

Bulimia is a search for solace. It organizes a retreat from the interpersonal world to a focus on the body. It is also a developmental retreat to earlier phases; it collapses structure into oral, anal, and genital metaphors in order to fill an inner emptiness that "combines qualities that are mouth-like, alimentary, and womb-like" (Hamburg 1989).

Jodie would complain of feeling so hungry that she couldn't fill herself up. She used the need for food to express her emptiness. She would complain, too, about feeling so full that she needed laxatives to empty herself. She used the need for laxatives to express the experience of bad feelings inside her. Her preoccupation with her bodily state prevented her from engaging in relationships and developing interpersonal skills. Perhaps this preoccupation kept her tied to her mother of infancy, when feeding and emptying were a primary way of relating.

Her parents were poor and lived in the city. Perhaps her father was elusive. At least she says she never got enough of him. Her mother wanted to live in the suburbs; she wanted to be thin but wasn't; she wishes she had had an opportunity for a college education. Her mother must have been unhappy. She was given to angry outbursts and threats of abandonment. One day she stormed out of the house and a terrified Jodie followed her, undiscovered, around the neighborhood. At the same time her mother was capable of warmth and generosity, and her unpredictability and inconsistency kept Jodie bound to her (Bergmann 1988).

Children acquiesce masochistically to mistreatment—its echo may be found in later behavior. Although Jodie was now in therapy as a young woman, she placed an advertisement in a singles newspaper and received numerous replies. She met many of the respondents, often giving them her home phone number. Once she came close to being raped. When this unsavory character called her back, she considered going out with him again. I told her how worried I was about this behavior. "Why would you offer yourself up to him as his next meal?" Jodie could take me in as a good mother, giving advice, or perhaps as a waitress serving her food.

After our first meeting, she dreamed the following: "I left work at 9 A.M. to go to lunch, and I stayed until noon. I felt guilty about taking three hours for lunch. When I woke up, I thought my guilt had to do with the fact that I wasn't doing my work." "Why did it take three hours?" I asked. She replied, "First we got lost. Then we couldn't get the waitress. It seemed like where I work, and it sometimes seemed like college. I was with my roommate and then with my boyfriend. I asked the waitress for the special. I think it was broiled fish, but she brought me a plate of bacon. I don't even eat bacon. I didn't want my boyfriend to pay but then I saw him take money from his wallet." In the dream, Jodie felt so hungry that she needed three hours for lunch. She experienced her relationship with the waitress/mother in terms of food. The waitress was going to bring her something special, but it quickly turned bad (into bacon).

Bulimia collapses relationships into an oral experience that fails because the food turns bad as soon as it is consumed.

Jodie had not mastered waiting. She yearned for immediate gratification, for that unknown something that she failed to get. Maybe, as Winnicott suggests, "Nothing happened when something might profitably have happened" (Winnicott 1974; quoted in Geist 1989, 10). I couldn't please her. She often told me, "Nothing is happening. You're not helping me. You talk too little. I need advice. You don't tell me anything I don't already know."

We first met in May 1980. She was a slim, boyish-looking woman of twenty-four. She came dressed in a sweat suit, with no makeup and very short hair. She apparently took no pains with her appearance. I was reminded that sometimes a demonstration of plainness exhibits innocence (Oliner 1988). I was the third therapist she had interviewed in as many weeks. She rejected the first for her condescending attitude; the second was fat. Her gaze made me feel uncomfortable. She was certainly examining the goods. I wondered if she had chosen me. She had. She continued to watch me closely. Some weeks later she complained angrily, "You said something last week that upset me. You said, 'I thought there were only three women in your group.' You looked angry, and I guess it's because I dramatize things that aren't important."

"I'm glad you brought this to my attention," I responded. "I wasn't aware of feeling angry and, in fact, I think you talk about important things in a way that minimizes their importance."

Jodie felt her vigilance had been rewarded. She had caught what she felt was an expression of anger on my face before I had had a chance to insult her verbally.

Thus an anal register of relationship—humiliation—had developed, and an effort to overcome it had been expressed by her burst of assertiveness.

After a year in treatment, Jodie was ten minutes late for a session. That was unusual. I went out to the waiting room and discovered that she was stuck in the elevator. She was screaming and crying. I called the fire department, and it took them twenty minutes to free her. I wanted to embrace her as a survivor of a horrible tragedy. It was a clear moment of affection that I felt for her, and that made me feel there was hope. I had become important to her and she to me. We went into my office for the few minutes remaining, and she asked me what I thought about her screaming and crying. I said it must have been awful. She said it was. Subsequently she told everyone the elevator story, including her mother, who responded, "What were you crying about? You knew the firemen would get you out." This experience had finally given Jodie the language to describe what had happened between them. She had grown to feel ashamed of her feelings.

Thus bulimia can collapse the world into anality. The world becomes an arena of shame and "shame becomes the agent that fragments the self" (Hamburg 1989).

She did not do her work. Even self-initiated projects were experienced as having been imposed by a frustrating other. She flirted with men at work, any man. One man asked her out, and she was flooded with excitement. She sought to masturbate, but this did not satisfy her; it turned her mood to irritation and anger. The adventures with men excited her needs and held the promise of filling her emptiness. But she was unprepared for the stimulation of feeling so much inside of her, and she immediately attempted to rid herself of the excitation.

Thus bulimia collapses the world into genitality, and excitement fills the emptiness, until that, too, fails and the empty feeling is soothed with food. But then the food turns bad as well and must be purged. Still the badness lingers.

She said she had been a chubby child and because of this was rejected by her peers. During adolescence, at her mother's urging, she had joined a particularly strict weight-loss program and had complied with the plan until she reduced her weight to 90 pounds. She was not able to sustain this weight and began to binge and purge, taking up to fifty laxatives a day. She would frequently get on her treadmill at 3 A.M. so she could exorcise her badness/fat before going to work. This effort was not just to exorcise the chubbiness, I thought. This was a child who had failed to thrive in social situations. Long ago, her incipient bulimia helped her organize her functioning by absorbing the outer world of people into the metaphoric language of food and weight.

During her two years with me, Jodie gained thirty pounds, a loving taking in and a hostile devouring of her analyst/mother. She always brought food or drink to sessions and then always dumped bottles or containers in the trash when she left. "This is where you come to be fed," I would say. She would reply, "Maybe." I would also comment, "You insist on eating in order to divest the session of any importance." She would counter, "You always think you're important." Clearly her body was the battleground. She made it into a fortress, a retreat from the anxiety aroused from relating to someone closely. During sessions, she would often ask me to lower the light and turn off the fan because the whirling blade agitated her. The first time the phone rang, she told me she knew it would. She was desperately trying to control my effect on her (Gonzales 1988; Boris 1988).

Toward the end, Jodie began leaving long messages on my answering machine. They did not require a response. Once I picked up the phone and she would not speak to me directly, only to the machine. She took to calling after midnight to avoid any danger of interruption or interaction. After several months of exploration and interpretation, I decided to use more active management. Now I said, "This must stop. You are giving everything away, and you will always remain innocent of experience. Hold on to it. Write it down. Learn from it. Don't purge it."

Jodie told me that when she was ten years old, she passed by her parents' bedroom and saw them having sex. She ran to the bathroom, crying. Her mother came after her. (I was reminded of the two masses of her dream separating.) Her mother warned her never to tell anyone what she had seen. (Purge it.) She still wondered why. But she had remained innocent of the wish to be sexually attractive and compete with her mother.

After my interpreting her excessive use of my answering machine, she felt injured. She told me, paradoxically, that this was the first meaningful statement I had made. Nevertheless she was leaving because she could not wait two years for the next bit of help. I commented, "I give you something good and then you leave." She stayed for a while. She bravely brought herself to sessions week after week until my summer vacation. At that last session she talked about feeling depressed. I suggested our upcoming separation as a cause. "Do all therapists have such big egos?" she asked. "Well, maybe it's just human to want to be important," she added. "For you, too?" I said. Jodie responded, "Yeah. I suppose so." "So, we want to be important to each other." She cried. It was a new sound, strange and clotted.

Jodie hasn't returned. The poignancy of bulimia is the search for solace that fails because, once found, the solace must be repudiated, like the food taken in as good, turns bad, and must be purged. She left a message on my machine telling me that she had no money and would not be coming back. She said, "It's been fun." It was never fun. I must content myself with having been around for only part of the work. Maybe the groundwork has been laid for the next phase.

Perhaps an aborted treatment was foreshadowed in the early dream material. Two masses separating represent her two sets of feelings about herself: the good baby and the kidneys that carry the badness. The dream also revealed that she felt our work held promise, that she would have a psychological birth. But she also anticipated that I would disappoint her because she couldn't wait. I wonder if Jodie had a fantasy that she was my unborn child. She panicked in the elevator, trapped, perhaps never to be born. By setting limits, I confronted Jodie's yearning for merger. I burst the bubble, and she had to run from the knowledge that she and I were separate.

Of course, more can be said about Jodie. There were achievements and fulfillments of varying degrees. She did have an area of excellent functioning. She did well in school and, while in treatment, earned her master's degree. Her professional life, however, was considerably impoverished and constantly disrupted by her interpersonal difficulties. I have often found significant ego fragmentation in eating disordered patients. Areas of good functioning may exist, but the part of the ego that is engaged in conflict is regressed and makes use of body orifices and processes to organize primitive symbolic communications.

I have selected one theme of a complex phenomenon, the collapse of structure, because this material was so compelling in Jodie's story. Because of the regressed nature of her functioning, the oral, anal, and genital worlds of supply, shame, and excitement became condensed and were blended in her behavioral language.

I could not inspire Jodie to behave less destructively or delay her search for instant solace. I hope that my appreciation of the value and the pain of her symptoms, and our struggle to understand her metaphoric communication, began for her the process of continued development. To paraphrase Winnicott, I hope something happened when it might profitably have happened.

References

Bergmann, M. V. 1988. "On Eating Disorders and Work Inhibition." In H. J. Schwartz, ed., *Bulimia: Psychoanalytic Treatment and Theory*. Madison, Conn.: International Universities Press.

Boris, H. N. 1988. "Torment of the Object: A Contribution to the Study of Bulimia." In H. J. Schwartz, ed., *Bulimia: Psychoanalytic Treatment and Theory*. Madison, Conn.: International Universities Press.

Ceasar, M. A. 1988. "Anorexia Nervosa and Bulimia: An Integrated Approach to Understanding and Treatment." In H. J. Schwartz, ed., *Bulimia: Psychoanalytic Treatment and Theory*. Madison, Conn.: International Universities Press.

Derrida, J. 1978. "Freud and the Scene of Writing." In *Writing and Difference*, trans. A. Bass. Chicago: University of Chicago Press.

Geist, Richard A. 1989. "Self Psychological Reflections on the Origins of Eating Disorders." *Journal of the American Academy of Psychoanalysis* 17 (1): 5–27.

Gesensway, D. B. 1988. "A Psychoanalytic Study of Bulimia and Pregnancy." In H. J. Schwartz, ed., *Bulimia: Psychoanalytic Treatment and Theory*. Madison, Conn.: International Universities Press.

Gonzalez, R. G. 1988. "Bulimia and Adolescence: Individual Psychoanalytic Treatment." In H. J. Schwarz, ed., *Bulimia: Psychoanalytic Treatment and Theory*. Madison, Conn.: International Universities Press.

Gould, S. J. 1991. "Grimm's Greatest Tale." In *Bully for Brontosaurus: Reflections in Natural History*. New York: Norton.

Hamburg, Paul. 1989. "Bulimia: The Construction of a Symptom." *Journal of the American Academy of Psychoanalysis* 17 (1): 131–40.

Krueger, D. 1988. "Body Self, Psychological Self, and Bulimia: Developmental and Clinical Considerations." In H. J. Schwartz, ed., *Bulimia: Psychoanalytic Treatment and Theory*. Madison, Conn.: International Universities Press.

Oliner, M. M. 1988. "Anal Components in Overeating." In H. J. Schwartz, ed., *Bulimia: Psychoanalytic Treatment and Theory*. Madison, Conn.: International Universities Press.

Winnicott, D. W. 1974. "Fear of Breakdown." *International Review of Psychoanalysis* 1:97–106.

8

Eating Disorders and Managed Care

INGE S. ORTMEYER

Managed care is a new factor in treatment considerations. Although medical treatment has always been attached to and/or predicated on payment, there have not always been regulations and approvals for care imposed by nonmedical sources. This phenomenon of corporate-driven care becomes a dynamic. In the best possible light, new and effective care may emerge within predetermined time parameters; but in the dimmer light are those patients who, because of restrictive limitations, receive partial or no treatment and thus do not recover. In our book, in which we discuss "new directions," it seemed essential that we note a factor that affects both patient and therapist. Inge Ortmeyer offers an overview in this chapter, raising some of the relevant issues that inevitably occur.

Barbara P. Kinoy, *Editor*

The nineties have witnessed a dramatic and revolutionary transformation of health care in the United States. In the wake of the public's rejection of President Clinton's proposals for universal health care and the single-payer model in the early nineties, there has been a radical takeover of health care by large corporate interests who consider health care a product and are driven by the demand for profits.

Managed behavioral health care is marketed as offering early detection of mental health problems, offering a broad range of services with continuity of care, reducing the cost borne by the patient, and improving the quality of care. In practice, however, managed care's essential economic basis as a business offering a product can decrease mental health care to a level insufficient for effective treatment, rendering undertreatment a critical issue. The use of gate-keepers (requiring referral by a primary physician or employee assistance program), restricting access to a selected panel of providers, requiring brief treatment and/or referral for medication, compromising patient privacy, and intruding into the patient-therapist relationship has severely affected the way clinicians associated with managed care organizations can treat their patients. Many practitioners who have elected to work outside managed care have suffered a reduction in their practices and incomes. Under managed care, "the patient/clinician dyad becomes a triad with the introduction of the managed care organization" (Wineburgh 1998, 433). Clinicians are required to submit their patients to preadmission screening, share highly sensitive information in treatment reports in the course of applying repeatedly for treatment authorizations, and indicate medication compliance. Approval of treatment plans is typically predicated on adherence to a computer-generated formula based on diagnosis. Wineburgh (1998) points out that ethical issues confronting a therapist working within managed behavioral health companies (MBHCs) include respect for the patient and the patient's autonomy, informed consent, confidentiality, divided loyalties, and the Hippocratic principle of *do no harm*.

Growth and consolidation of MBHCs have been enormous. In 1992, 78 million people were enrolled in them; by 1998, the number of enrollees had grown to 156 million people. Most of the growth has been in capitated behavioral health "carve-outs," whereby a separate company from the medical Health Maintenance Organization (HMO), managed care, or insurance plan is paid to provide behavioral health for a fixed price and in employee assistance programs. Takeovers have concentrated 84 percent of the marketplace in the top twelve programs, with 60 percent in the top three. "Mergers have created debt-strapped Goliaths eager to cut costs and curtail services" reads the subhead of an April 1999 article in *NASW News*, a publication of the National Association of Social Workers (O'Neill 1999).

Eating disorders have been particularly affected by managed behavioral health care because of the frequent need for extended treatment and because of efforts to trivialize or blame the individual for her disorder. Seriously ill patients suffering from the ravages of eating disorders are considered self-destructive and not worth the expense of adequate hospitalization. Arnold Andersen (1998) notes that along with some positive trends, there "have been predatory, irresponsible changes based on the assumption that health care is simply a business commodity." The splitting of the medical and psychiatric components of eating disorders and the underfunding of the latter has deprived patients of vital care. Legislation to provide parity in coverage for psychiatric and medical disorders was passed by Congress in 1996 but has been restricted to certain illnesses, and these do not include eating disorders.

Federal legislation, namely, the ERISA (Employment Retirement Income Security Act), was enacted in 1974 in response to concern that corrupt, incompetent pension managers were mismanaging the self-funded employee benefit plans entrusted to them,, including retirement and health insurance. When passed, ERISA had no connection to malpractice liability. Whereas clinicians can be sued for compensatory damages in malpractice suits, the law has shielded HMOs who can only be sued for medical costs amounting to far less than could be recovered under punitive damages. The *New York Times* (Pear 1998) reported that both judges and legislators have become concerned about the failures of ERISA to protect consumers and sufficiently punish organizations that are found negligent in denying care. For instance, because of ERISA, one federal court noted that, in the event of a suicide following a denial of psychiatric care, family members could not sue the HMO or insurance company for wrongful death.

In order to justify payment for treatment of psychiatric disorders, managed care companies demand considerable information about the nature and severity of the disorders as well as the degree to which the patient's functioning is impaired. Patients and their treaters are assured that such information shall be privileged and confidential. In practice, however, according to many reports, widespread and flagrant violations of confidentiality take place. Frequently employers receive reports from insurance companies and managed care organizations about their employees' medical and psychiatric care. Whereas it is illegal to use health data in hiring and firing people, it is not illegal to have such information and to use it in undisclosed ways. Medical records, like financial profiles and buying habits, have become a hot commodity to be cataloged and traded like baseball cards. One of my recovered patients was refused life insurance because the company had discovered that she had been treated for bulimia. Many people would rather pay for their treatment or forego treatment rather than have an eating disorder diagnosis on their claim form. A number of practitioners have opted to work outside the managed care system and negotiate fees with their patients rather than share privileged information and be subjected to the arbitrary control of managed care.

Kathryn Zerbe (1996) advocates forming an alliance with the managed care case manager that involves sharing as many details as possible about eating disorders, including critical information, so that the treatment can be supported. On occasion, she sends articles to the case manager documenting statistics and research trends. Cost-offset data and outcome data can also be persuasive. Zerbe describes a case in which the patient became her own advocate with the case manager. She underscored that, "in the current age, clinicians must work with the case management process until a better, more direct way is found to adjudicate claims." While the system of payment for medical care goes through the present transition, practitioners and patients are faced with having to accommodate to a system which, in many ways, is seriously flawed. Often practitioners now find it necessary to intervene and to become advocates on behalf of their patients (Andersen 1998, 277). It is hoped that through the efforts of citizens and the government a sound and equitable system for the payment of medical care emerges in the new century.

References

Andersen, Arnold E. 1998. "Treatment of Eating Disorders in the Context of Managed Care in the United States: A Clinician's Perspective." In Walter Vandereycken and Pierre J. V. Beaumont, eds., *Treating Eating Disorders: Ethical, Legal and Personal Issues*, 261–82. London: Athlone.

O'Neill, John. 1999. "At Managed Care's Table, Physical Care Takes Lion's Share: Psychosocial Care Often Left with Crumbs." *National Association of Social Work News* 44, no. 4 (April): 3.

Pear, Robert. 1998. "Hands Tied, Judges Rue Law That Limits HMO Liability." *New York Times*, July 11, A1.

Wineburgh, Marsha. 1998. "Ethics, Managed Care, and Outpatient Psychotherapy." *Clinical Social Work Journal* 15, no. 4: 433–43.

Zerbe, Kathryn J. 1996. "Extending the Frame: Working with Managed Care to Support Treatment for a Refractory Patient." In Joellen Werne, ed., *Treating Eating Disorders*, 335–56. San Francisco: Jossey-Bass.

9

Cognitive-Behavioral Therapy and Other Short-Term Approaches in the Treatment of Eating Disorders

JAMES T. WEGNER AND ANDREA Z. WEGNER

Over the past fifteen years significant strides have been made in identifying, developing, and implementing therapeutic strategies used in the treatment of eating disorders. At the same time, the exigencies of providing psychiatric treatment in this era of managed heath care have necessitated finding clinically effective, yet cost-effective, short-term approaches. One treatment that has emerged is cognitive-behavioral therapy (CBT), and a growing body of empirical evidence has clearly demonstrated its effectiveness in the treatment of bulimia nervosa (Agras et al. 1992; Fairburn, Agras, and Wilson 1992; Garner et al. 1993) and binge eating disorder (Agras et al. 1997). Moreover, although initially thought to be an ineffective therapeutic approach for anorexia nervosa, a number of recent articles have suggested that, with modification, CBT can be successfully used in treating anorexia as well (e.g., Garner, Vitousek, and Pike 1997). This chapter describes cognitive-behavioral therapy, along with other current short-term treatments for eating disorders.

COGNITIVE-BEHAVIORAL THERAPY AND BULIMIA NERVOSA

Cognitive-behavioral therapy was first introduced by Beck and his colleagues (1979) and was initially used in the treatment of depression. The use of CBT in bulimia nervosa was first conceptualized by Fairburn (1981), and over the years a detailed and periodically revised treatment manual has evolved (Fairburn, Marcus, and Wilson 1993), which has given clinicians a blueprint for treating eating disorders using this approach.

The CBT model emphasizes that both cognitive and behavioral factors are at play in maintaining bingeing behavior. Since bulimics overvalue body weight and shape, the stage is set for the individual to restrict food intake in order to attain or maintain the goal of the desired physical appearance. This restriction then leads to being susceptible to loss of control over eating, which results in bingeing.

Self-induced vomiting and other forms of inappropriate weight control attempt to compensate for the calories consumed during the binge. The purging behaviors persist because they lessen the anxiety surrounding weight gain. However, as a result of the binge/purge behavior, the patient feels guilty and suffers from a compromised sense of self. This model for bulimia nervosa suggests that treatment must not only address the presenting behaviors of binge eating and purging but must also assist the patient in replacing dietary restriction with a more normal eating pattern. In addition, it must also help modify the dysfunctional thinking and feelings regarding the significance of body shape and weight (Wilson, Fairburn, and Agras 1997).

PRELIMINARY CONSIDERATIONS

Although CBT has demonstrated a high degree of efficacy in treatment outcome studies, certain cohorts of patients would not be considered suitable candidates for therapy (see, e.g., chapter 11 below). Co-morbidity of substance abuse or dependence would preclude a patient from CBT, as would a concurrent diagnosis of severe depression (Agras and Apple 1997). These conditions would interfere with the patient's ability to adhere to the treatment program; so before attempting CBT, it is preferable to begin therapy by treating the underlying addiction or mood disorder first.

Treatment typically lasts about twenty weeks and consists of nineteen sessions. CBT has three clearly delineated stages: Stages 1 and 2 consist of eight sessions each, and Stage 3 is three sessions. Each session lasts up to fifty minutes, and the therapist adheres strictly to the time frame of sessions.

CBT focuses on the present and the future, and is semi-structured and problem-oriented in nature. As with all therapy formats, a good therapist-patient relationship is essential for recovery. The patient has an active role in the treatment sessions, and the success of CBT depends considerably on the patient's ability to remain motivated to follow through on homework assignments. The therapist has an active voice in the sessions and provides didactic information, support, guidance, and encouragement. Before beginning Stage 1, a thorough psychiatric evaluation should be completed to assess the patient's suitability for the CBT program.

Stage 1 (Sessions 1–8)

The two major aims of Stage 1 include orienting the patient to the cognitive-behavioral approach and replacing the binge/purge behaviors with a more stable pattern of eating. In outlining the rationale underlying the CBT approach to treatment, the therapist explains the vicious cycle that occurs within the constellation of bulimic symptoms and their interrelationships (strict dieting, bingeing and purging, extreme concern about weight and shape, and low self-esteem), and how it perpetuates the eating disorder. In the first session the therapist also introduces self-monitoring. The patient is instructed to keep a record on a daily food record sheet of everything she eats. The time of day, the food eaten, whether a binge or purge occurred, and the associated thoughts and feelings are all noted and then discussed with the therapist in the following session. The self-monitoring serves two purposes: (1) It provides data for the therapist regarding the patient's eating style and concomitant emotional states; and (2) it increases the patient's awareness of what is being eaten and under what conditions. In addition to self-monitoring, the patient is also instructed to weigh herself once a week.

During Sessions 3 to 8, the therapist introduces behavioral strategies that are geared toward regaining control over eating. These strategies include self-control and stimulus control. In the first session, the patient is asked to identify high-risk situations that may trigger a binge and then to make a list of alternative activities that are enjoyable and feasible but at the same time incompatible with binge eating. These behaviors may include talking with a friend on the phone, taking a shower, walking, or going to a store. Stimulus control is a technique whereby the patient attempts to control the environment by imposing certain rules about eating. Such measures would include restricting eating to one part of the house, limiting the quantity of binge foods in the house, practicing leaving food on the plate, avoiding food shopping when hungry, and always using a shopping list. This self-control technique is especially helpful in the early stages of treatment, when impulse control is somewhat tenuous.

Educating the patient about weight and eating is another task that is completed in Stage 1 of CBT treatment. Areas discussed include body weight and the concept of the body mass index, the physical consequences of dieting, laxative use, and self-induced vomiting (and their ineffectiveness in regulating weight), and the adverse effects of dieting. This didactic approach is critical as it dispels the myths patients frequently have concerning eating and body weight, and lays the groundwork for altering the patient's perceptions and cognitive beliefs about food. In addition, the patient is asked to restrict eating to three meals and two or three snacks per day. This eating-by-the-clock strategy is employed to disrupt the cycle of overeating followed by food restriction that so frequently characterizes the bulimic's eating habits.

In a high percentage of patients, Stage 1 results in a significant reduction in the frequency of binge eating and purging. If, however, binge eating continues to occur at least once a day, then Stage 1 should be extended. If significant improvement has not occurred by Session 8, then this approach should be stopped and another therapeutic model introduced.

Stage 2 (Sessions 9–16)

While continuing to discuss the importance of regular eating patterns, the review of the monitoring sheets, weekly weighing, and the use of self-control and stimulus-control techniques, Stage 2 begins to address dieting in general, concerns about body shape, and the cognitive distortions that accompany bulimia nervosa. The sessions shift toward a more cognitive focus and include training the patient to problem-solve everyday situations that contribute to the continuation of bulimia symptomatology.

By the beginning of Stage 2, the patient has become acquainted with the notion that rigid dieting predisposes the individual to binge eating. The next step is to assist the patient in identifying what foods are eaten and how much is consumed. The patient is asked to generate a list of foods to be avoided and put them in rank order. During Stage 2 the patient should progressively reintroduce these "forbidden foods" into her diet, beginning with the least objectionable ones. The goal of this exercise is to demonstrate to the patient that a reasonable degree of control can be attained over foods considered frightening. Restriction of the total amount eaten is addressed in a manner similar to that for avoiding certain foods. Through careful assessment of the monitoring sheets, it can be determined whether the patient is eating too little. If this is the case, the patient should be urged to consume at least 1,500 calories a day.

As binge-eating episodes become intermittent, the patient and therapist then must identify the precipitants or triggers for bingeing. These may include interpersonal difficulties, self-esteem deficits, mood disturbances, or even specific thoughts. Once they are identified, CBT is designed to allow the patient to develop behavioral and cognitive skills for coping more effectively with these situations without the need to rely on bingeing and purging. This is accomplished by the therapist assisting the patient in improving her problem-solving skills using a seven-step process (see Fairburn, Marcus, and Wilson 1993), which first identifies the problem, considers the various possible solutions, and then assesses the feasibility of each solution. Once a solution is settled on, the steps needed to carry it out are defined and then acted on. Finally, the day after the solution has been carried out, the patient scrutinizes the entire sequence and evaluates the success or failure of the endeavor. The goal of this therapeutic task is to assist the patient in developing a framework for problem-solving skills that can be implemented whenever difficulties arise.

One of the most common triggers for inducing binge eating is disordered thinking (e.g., believing you are overweight when you are not or believing a five-pound weight gain will be evident to everyone). Often, however, the patient remains unaware of the thinking patterns that contribute to the onset of a binge episode. At this juncture in treatment, the therapist begins to address the underlying problematic thoughts and attitudes that perpetuate the eating disorder. The patient's concern about shape and weight is especially susceptible to faulty cognitive patterns such as dichotomous thinking (something is either all good or all bad, nothing in between). Other types of disordered thinking frequently seen in eating disorder patients include overgeneralization, catastrophizing, selective abstraction, and magnifying negatives and minimizing positives (Agras and Apple 1997). Dysfunctional attitudes are also a critical aspect of the psychological landscape that contribute to maintaining eating disordered behavior. Often the bulimic patient believes that in order to be happy, successful, and attractive, you must be thin. If you are fat, then you are depressed, viewed as a failure, and ugly. These aberrant thinking and attitudinal styles are confronted in CBT treatment using cognitive restructuring techniques (see Hawton et al. 1989).

The patient is asked to identify a problematic thought that she believes may contribute to the binge-eating disturbance. The thought itself is noted and written down, followed by objective evidence to support and refute that thought. The therapist assists the patient in developing a reasonable conclusion based on their exploration of the evidence. Finally, the patient determines a course of action that will direct the behavior.

Stage 3 (Sessions 17–19)

The third stage, when sessions are biweekly, focuses on strategies to prevent relapse. The major goal is for the patient to learn how to anticipate future difficulties and apply both the problem-solving and cognitive restructuring skills that have been acquired in order to circumvent a recurrence of binge/purge behaviors. At the same time, however, it is important that the therapist point out to the patient that under severe stress, binge-eating behaviors may be revisited but can be viewed as lapses rather than a full-blown relapse. In addition, each patient completes a written maintenance plan that can be followed once therapy has ended.

COGNITIVE-BEHAVIORAL THERAPY AND
BINGE-EATING DISORDERS

Although binge-eating disorder was first described by Stunkard in 1959, it only became part of the official psychiatric nomenclature when, in 1994, it was included in Appendix B of the fourth edition of the *Diagnostic and Statistical Manual* (*DSM-IV*) as an example of an eating disorder not otherwise specified. A number of controlled studies have examined the efficacy of cognitive-behavioral therapy in this patient group and have found that it is a beneficial therapeutic approach in the reduction of binge-eating episodes (Agras et al. 1997; Marcus, Wing, and Fairburn 1995; Peterson et al. 1998). Frequently a group format is used in treating obese patients. Therapists need to modify the CBT treatment when working with patients with binge-eating disorder. Such patients tend to gain weight during CBT treatment; to prevent this, some weight-control measures, along with a mild exercise program, need to be incorporated into the first phase of treatment and is monitored throughout the course of therapy (Agras and Apple 1997). Second, while the bulimic patient's main goal is to stop binge eating, the obese patient primarily enters treatment to lose weight. Thus the therapist must emphasize that the primary goal is the cessation of binge eating and establishing a healthier eating style. Further, the patient must understand that more important than reaching any goal weight is the need to develop control over binge eating in order to diminish the feeling of being out of control and reduce a preoccupation with food. Not all obese patients are able to conceptualize the importance of working toward a different attitude while not losing weight.

COGNITIVE-BEHAVIORAL THERAPY AND
ANOREXIA NERVOSA

Many psychological characteristics are common to both anorexia and bulimia nervosa. These include weight preoccupation, perfectionistic tendencies, starvation symptoms, and faulty cognitive patterns. Presumably, then, CBT should also be an effective treatment for anorexia nervosa. A number of early reports (e.g., Garner and Bemis 1982) had suggested that CBT might be an effective treatment for anorexia nervosa. However, Cooper and Fairburn (1984), while reporting some success with anorexics who binged and purged, found that the restricting subtype fared poorly with CBT. These early reports were anecdotal clinical case studies that lacked the methodological rigor of controlled clinical trials. One reason for a dearth of research in this area could be that the incidence of anorexia nervosa is quite low, making it more difficult to gather a cohort large enough to undergo statistical analysis. Another issue lies in the fact that the treatment of choice for the extreme low-weight anorexic is typically hospitalization. Thus a therapeutic program devised for outpatients would have to preclude the more chronic anorexic patient and would affect the generalizability of the results across the symptom severity continuum.

Recently attempts have been made to describe a CBT treatment approach for anorexic patients (Garner, Vitousek, and Pike 1997), and clinical trials are presently under way to evaluate the efficacy of CBT in anorexia nervosa.

Two major issues complicate CBT treatment in anorexic patients that are absent in bulimia nervosa. These include the level of motivation for therapeutic help and addressing the issue of weight and weight gain in treatment (Garner, Vitousek, and Pike 1997). Although motivating eating disorder patients can be problematic, it is especially arduous with the anorexic. The vast majority of anorexic patients will resist gaining weight, though this is the main goal of treatment for them. Thus the initial phase of CBT must incorporate a substantial amount of time devoted to developing and sustaining motivation for change.

In CBT, the bulimic patient is reassured that weight gain, if any, would be minimal, thus reducing the fear of becoming fat. However, since the major goal in treating the anorexic is to gain weight, the patient must deal with the fear of becoming fat while actually becoming fatter (Garner, Vitousek, and Pike 1997). This issue can and does have a devastating effect on motivational levels and may prompt the patient to terminate treatment prematurely. The therapist must constantly address this concern, as it can quickly sabotage the therapy.

The bulimic patient is entrusted with the task of self-weighing on a weekly basis. However, the anorexic must be regularly checked by the therapist or nutritionist, so that weight goals are carefully monitored.

Although the bulimic patient is introduced to the concept of self-monitoring at the first session, the anorexic needs to be gradually exposed to this therapeutic task. This is because initially the anorexic is disinterested in progress, since that requires gaining weight. Further, the anorexic may require meal planning in order to structure her food intake.

The social dysfunction that often accompanies anorexia nervosa, the frequent need for family involvement, particularly with young anorexic patients, and a longer duration of therapy (the anorexic patient may remain in CBT treatment for one to two years), have contributed to an interweaving of cognitive-behavioral and interpersonal approaches in working with this patient population (Garner, Vitousek, and Pike 1997). (See chapter 11 for examples of interweaving approaches.)

Other treatment differences between the anorexic and bulimic patient include a focus on the medical risks and the psychobiology of starvation associated with anorexia nervosa during the educative aspects of CBT. In addition, the longer treatment duration is required because of motivational issues. However, the bulimic patient is also at risk (see chapter 1 above). Both anorexic and bulimic patients require ongoing medical evaluation and surveillance as part of the treatment plan. Typically sessions are scheduled twice weekly for Stage 1 of treatment (the first month), whereas Stage 2 has weekly sessions that can last for as long as a year. Stage 3 usually lasts six months, at which time the frequency of appointments is first biweekly and then monthly.

INTERPERSONAL PSYCHOTHERAPY AND
EATING DISORDERS

Like cognitive-behavioral therapy, interpersonal psychotherapy (IPT) was initially developed for the treatment of nonpsychotic depression in an outpatient setting (Klerman et al. 1984). The major underlying assumption of IPT is that the development of clinical depression occurs in a social and interpersonal context and that the onset, response to treatment, and outcome are influenced by the interpersonal relations between the depressed patient and significant others (Klerman and Weissman 1993). These authors stress that there is no assumption that interpersonal difficulties cause depression but rather that the depression occurs within an interpersonal context. The therapeutic strategies of IPT are designed to assist the patient in dealing more effectively with interpersonal dysfunction.

Four interpersonal problem areas have been identified. The most common difficulties are role disputes and are typically seen in married couples. Role transition is another area and often takes the form of problems resulting from separating from parents and adjusting to life away from home or difficulty adjusting to marriage or parenthood. Unresolved grief is another interpersonal conflict area. Interpersonal deficits, characterized by an inability to form or maintain intimate relationships (often seen in schizoid individuals) is the fourth conflict area.

Fairburn (1993) adapted IPT for the treatment of bulimia nervosa. The only modifications included an assessment of the eating disorder in the first stage of treatment and a limitation to a total of nineteen sessions. It is interesting to note that after the eating disorder was discussed in the initial sessions (and the discussion centers on the relationship between interpersonal events and the bulimic behavior), it was essentially ignored throughout the remainder of therapy, and the focus of treatment concerned the interpersonal realm. Fairburn and colleagues (1991) found that at one-year follow-up, IPT was as successful a treatment for bulimia nervosa as was CBT. This finding was also replicated in a study of binge-eating disorder using IPT and CBT in a group treatment setting (Wilfrey et al. 1993). These results clearly demonstrate how profound an impact interpersonal dysfunction has on the maintenance of these disorders. It is also noteworthy that the onset of many eating disorders is often during adolescence, a developmental period in an individual's life heavily laden with issues surrounding interpersonal relationships. Thus it is not surprising that IPT is an effective treatment format for binge-eating disorders, since it addresses some underlying interpersonal issues that might have contributed to the development of eating problems.

OTHER SHORT-TERM PSYCHOLOGICAL TREATMENTS

Another treatment approach used for bulimia nervosa is response prevention (Leitenberg et al. 1988), a behavior therapy that has its roots in flooding and implosion techniques. In this treatment the patient binges during the course of a therapy session until the desire to purge occurs. The patient then remains in session until that urge dissipates, demonstrating that control over purging can occur. The underlying assumption is that once the patient's desire to purge has been eliminated, binge-eating episodes will be reduced. While the initial study showed some promise in the technique (although patients found the procedure quite disturbing), later work (Agras et al. 1989) demonstrated that adding response prevention to CBT led to poorer results than when CBT was used alone.

Another therapeutic approach used with binge-eating disorders is psychoeducational group therapy. This modality is primarily a stripped-down version of CBT, since it only includes the psychoeducational aspects. In a group format, patients receive education in the areas of nutrition, the adverse effects of dieting, bingeing and purging, and sometimes include discussion on the cognitive distortions that frequently occur in eating disorder patients. It is usually a very brief intervention (up to five sessions) and has shown some success (see Olmstead et al. 1991) in patients with mild binge-eating disturbances.

Self-help manuals, using a CBT approach to binge eating difficulties, have also been developed. This format sometimes includes a therapist-led discussion on the use of the manual. Other versions have no guided assistance. In the initial study, Cooper, Coker, and Fleming (1994) showed that more than half the bulimic patients reported marked clinical improvement using a therapist-led, self-help manual.

With the advent of managed health care, impetus has developed in our field to identify the most cost-effective and easily disseminated forms of treatment. Fairburn and Peveler (1990) have suggested the adoption of a stepped-care approach in the treatment of binge-eating disorders. This health care delivery model involves first offering a simple treatment, since some patients will respond positively. The first treatment tier might be an unsupervised self-help format. Those who do not respond move on to the next step, which involves more intensive therapy. For example, it might consist of a guided self-help treatment. Should self-help prove unsuccessful, then the third level of care, such as a CBT approach, would be required. If the patient proves to be a nonresponder, then another level of treatment would be instituted, such as the addition of an antidepressant, partial hospitalization, or an inpatient stay. Recent research has shown that this model may be promising for both bulimia nervosa (Davis et al. 1999) and binge-eating disorders (Peterson et al. 1998). Of particular importance at this juncture, however, is for researchers to identify patient characteristics that may predict the level of stepped-up care to which the individual will respond.

CONCLUDING REMARKS

The efficacy of cognitive-behavioral therapy and interpersonal psychotherapy has been clearly demonstrated in the treatment of binge-eating disorders. Furthermore, initial clinical studies have been encouraging for the use of CBT in treating anorexia nervosa as well, and controlled clinical trials are currently under way.

Since cognitive-behavioral therapy and interpersonal psychotherapy are both manualized treatments, they have the added advantage of being widely available to clinicians and easier for experienced therapists to acquire the skills needed to use these approaches. Moreover, since these approaches are highly structured and have time limits, both clinician and patient are forced to remain focused on a circumscribed set of symptoms and behaviors, and to work hard on making well-defined changes. All these features are especially attractive given the reality of managed care and the corresponding need for adequate and effective treatment within that circumscribed framework.

References

Agras, W. S. and R. F. Apple. 1997. *Overcoming Eating Disorders: A Cognitive-Behavioral Treatment for Bulimia Nervosa and Binge-Eating Disorder. Therapist Guide*. San Antonio: The Psychological Corporation.

Agras, W. S., E. M. Rossiter, B. Arnow, J. A. Schneider, C. F. Telch, S. D. Raeburn, B. Bruce, M. Perl, and L. M. Koran. 1992. "Pharmacologic and Cognitive-Behavioral Treatment for Bulimia Nervosa: A Controlled Comparison." *American Journal of Psychiatry* 149:82–87.

Agras, W. S., J. A. Schneider, B. Arnow, S. D. Raeburn, and C. F. Telch. 1989. "Cognitive-Behavioral and Response Prevention Treatments for Bulimia Nervosa." *Journal of Consulting and Clinical Psychology* 57:215–21.

Agras, W. S., C. F. Telch, B. Arnow, D. Eldredge, and M. Marnell. 1997. "One-Year Follow-up of Cognitive-Behavioral Therapy for Obese Individuals with Binge Eating Disorder." *Journal of Consulting and Clinical Psychology* 65:343–47.

Beck, A. T., A. J. Rush, B. F. Shaw, and G. Emery. 1979. *Cognitive Therapy of Depression*. New York: Guilford.

Cooper, P. J., S. Coker, and C. Fleming. 1994. "Self-Help for Bulimia Nervosa: A Preliminary Report." *International Journal of Eating Disorders* 16:401–4.

Cooper, P. J., and C. G. Fairburn. 1984. "Cognitive-Behavioral Treatment of Anorexia Nervosa: Some Preliminary Findings." *Journal of Psychosomatic Research* 28:493–99.

Davis, R., G. McVey, M. Heinmaa, W. Rockert, and S. Kennedy. 1999. "Sequencing of Cognitive-Behavioral Treatments for Bulimia Nervosa." *International Journal of Eating Disorders* 25:361–74.

Diagnostic and Statistical Manual of Mental Disorders (IV). 1994. Washington, D.C.: American Psychiatric Association.

Fairburn, C. G. 1981. "A Cognitive Behavioural Approach to the Management of Bulimia." *Psychological Medicine* 11:707–11.

————. 1993. "Interpersonal Psychotherapy for Bulimia Nervosa. In G. L. Klerman and M. M. Weissman, eds., *New Applications of Interpersonal Psychotherapy*, 353–78. Washington, D.C.: American Psychiatric Press.

Fairburn, C. G., W. S. Agras, and G. T. Wilson. 1992. "The Research on the Treatment of Bulimia Nervosa: Practical and Theoretical Implications. In G. H. Anderson and S. H. Kennedy, eds., *The Biology of Feast and Famine: Relevance to Eating Disorders*, 317–40. New York: Academic Press.

Fairburn, C. G., R. Jones, R. C. Peveler, S. J. Carr, R. A. Solomon, M. E. O'Connor, J. Burton, and R. A. Hope. 1991. "Three Psychological Treatments for Bulimia Nervosa." *Archives of General Psychiatry* 48:463–69.

Fairburn, C. G., M. D. Marcus, and G. T. Wilson. 1993. Cognitive-Behavior Therapy for Binge Eating and Bulimia Nervosa: A Comprehensive Treatment Manual." In C. G. Fairburn and G. T. Wilson, eds., *Binge Eating: Nature, Assessment, and Treatment*, 361–404. New York: Guilford.

Fairburn, C. G., and R. C. Peveler. 1990. "Bulimia Nervosa and a Stepped Care Approach to Management." *Gut* 31:1220–22.

Garner, D. M., and K. M. Bemis. 1982. "A Cognitive-Behavioral Approach to Anorexia Nervosa." *Cognitive Therapy and Research* 6:123–50.

Garner, D. M., W. Rockert, R. Davis, M. V. Garner, M. P. Olmstead, and M. Eagle. 1993. "Comparison between Cognitive-Behavioral and Supportive-Expressive Therapy for Bulimia Nervosa." *American Journal of Psychiatry* 150:37–46.

Garner, D. M., K. M. Vitousek, and K. M. Pike. 1997. "Cognitive-Behavioral Therapy for Anorexia Nervosa." In D. M. Garner and P. E. Garfinkel, eds., *Handbook of Treatment for Anorexia Nervosa and Bulimia*, 67–144. New York: Guilford.

Hawton, K., P. M. Salkovskis, J. Kirk, and D. M. Clark. 1989. *Cognitive Behavior Therapy for Psychiatric Problems: A Practical Guide*. Oxford: Oxford University Press.

Klerman, G. L., and M. M. Weissman. 1993. "Interpersonal Psychotherapy for Depression: Background and Concepts." In G. L. Klerman and M. M. Weissman, eds., *New Applications of Interpersonal Psychotherapy*, 3–26. Washington, D.C.: American Psychiatric Press.

Klerman, G. L., M. M. Weissman, B. J. Rounsaville, and E. S. Chevron, 1984. *Interpersonal Psychotherapy of Depression*. New York: Basic Books.

Leitenberg, H., J. Rosen, J. Gross, S. Nudelman, and I. Vara. 1988. "Exposure Plus Response-Prevention Treatment of Bulimia Nervosa." *Journal of Consulting and Clinical Psychology* 56:535–41.

Marcus, M. D., R. R. Wing, and C. G. Fairburn. 1995. "Cognitive Treatment of Binge Eating versus Behavioral Weight Control in the Treatment of Binge Eating Disorder." *Annals of Behavioral Medicine* 17:5090.

Olmstead, M. P., R. Davis, D. M. Garner, W. Rockert, M. J. Irvine, and M. Eagle. 1991. "Efficacy of a Brief Group Psychoeducational Intervention of Bulimia Nervosa. *Behaviour Research and Psychotherapy* 29:79–83.

Peterson, C. B., J. E. Mitchell, S. Engbloom, S. Nugent, M. P. Mussell, and J. P. Miller. 1998. Group Cognitive-Behavioral Treatment of Binge Eating Disorder: A Comparison of Therapist-Led versus Self-Help Formats. *International Journal of Eating Disorders* 24:125–36.

Stunkard, A. J. 1959. "Eating Patterns and Obesity." *Psychiatric Quarterly* 33:284–92.

Wilfrey, D. E., W. S. Agras, C. F. Telch, E. M. Rossiter, J. A. Schneider, A. G. Cole, I. A. Sifford, and S. D. Raeburn. 1993. "Group Cognitive-Behavioral Therapy and Group Interpersonal Psychotherapy for the Nonpurging Bulimic Individual: A Controlled Comparison." *Journal of Consulting and Clinical Psychology* 61:296–305.

Wilson, G. T., C. G. Fairburn, and W. S. Agras. 1997. "Cognitive-Behavioral Therapy for Bulimia Nervosa." In D. M. Garner and P. E. Garfinkel, eds., *Handbook of Treatment of Anorexia Nervosa and Bulimia*, 67–93. New York: Guilford.

10

The Nurse's Role in a Pilot Program Using a Modified Cognitive-Behavioral Approach

PHYLLIS ROLOFF

Cognitive-behavioral therapy (CBT) and high-dose fluoxetine (Prozac) have both been proven to benefit patients with bulimia. In spite of that, only a small fraction of bulimic patients actually receive these treatments, as they have been limited to certain psychiatric settings. Many people do not have such facilities in their area or lack the insurance or finances to use them or feel embarrassed to go for psychiatric care. If these treatments could be delivered effectively by medical doctors and nurses in primary care settings, then they would be available to vastly more patients.

In 1997 the National Institute of Health provided a federal grant to study the delivery of treatments for bulimia in a primary care setting. The principal investigators are Dr. B. Timothy Walsh, professor of psychiatry at the College of Physicians and Surgeons, Columbia University; director of Eating Disorders Research Unit, New York State Psychiatric Institute; and an expert in the use of medication to treat eating disorders; and Dr. Christopher Fairburn, Department of Psychiatry, University of Oxford, England, a pioneer in the treatment of eating disorders and in the development of CBT in treating bulimia. The co-investigator is Dr. Diane Mickley, an authority on medical care of eating disorders and director of the Wilkins Center for Eating Disorders. The grant provides for four months of free treatment for two hundred women with bulimia in a primary care setting through Glenville

Medical Associates in Greenwich, Connecticut. All patients receive medication (half receive placebo, half receive fluoxetine) and medical care from the physicians in the group. Half the patients also receive CBT working with nurses in the practice.

Wilkins Center has been actively involved in this project. The role of the nurse is central to this study, and Phyllis Roloff RN, director of Nursing at Wilkins Center, has played a pivotal role. Ms. Roloff treated a series of Wilkins Center patients with CBT to pilot the nurse's role. Once the NIH (National Institute of Health) study began, she helped the Glenville nursing staff to understand and provide CBT to bulimic patients. She coordinated medical care for the study patients at Glenville with the collection of research data to evaluate benefits and arranged aftercare for patients from the study who wished further treatment. In the following, Ms. Roloff describes her experience as a nurse doing CBT.

—Diane W. Mickley, M.D.

As I approached the room to meet my first CBT patient I was both excited about this new responsibility and apprehensive about how we would work together and whether I was equipped to do this. As it turned out, she was experiencing the same feelings. And thus we began.

I explained that this was a self-help program, and I was there to guide and encourage her and to answer any questions she might have.

The following is a summary of my role, as a nurse, in a modified cognitive-behavioral therapy program. This treatment approach is based on a book by Dr. Christopher Fairburn (1995). This program is suggested for *very carefully selected* patients, and should not, Dr. Fairburn cautions, be used by anyone who is underweight, has a serious physical illness or whose physical health is being affected by bingeing (unless the physician grants permission), is pregnant, is significantly depressed or demoralized, and, finally, who has general problems with impulse control, such as alcohol or drug abuse and/or repeated self-harming behavior (137). The first half of the book is educational; the second half describes the actual program.

I have discovered that patients I have worked with found the first half most interesting and informative, not at all the boring text they expected.

The first topic covered is bingeing. The characteristics of a binge are described, including feelings, speed of eating, agitation, secretiveness, and loss of control. Examples of the kinds of food eaten and different types of binges are given. He describes obesity, bulimia, and anorexia. He discusses dieting and its effects. He touches on the use of laxatives, vomiting, diet pills, diuretics, and excessive exercise. He addresses concerns of physical appearance and weight, moods, and relationships. Dr. Fairburn also describes personality characteristics generally seen in binge-eaters. Patients, when reading this section, often feel that he is describing them personally.

A chapter is devoted to the physical problems associated with bingeing, purging, and dieting, such as damage to tooth enamel, electrolyte imbalance, tears in the esophagus, and infertility. The last chapters in this section are devoted to discussions of known and suspected causes of binge eating, as well as binge eating as an addiction. Various treatment modalities are reviewed.

The six steps in the program set forth by Dr. Fairburn are aimed at behavioral changes. The first is that of record keeping, that is, careful notation of food eaten, how, when, and what, with accompanying remarks about feelings. Most people who have sought treatment for their eating disorder are familiar with this exercise, and some find it quite difficult. Facing, in black and white, exactly what they have been eating and why is extremely painful and hard to accept. The nurse's nonjudgmental acceptance is extremely important. I emphasize that record keeping is not a punishment but a goal to reveal any pattern that may exist; for example, a particular person or situation may repeatedly trigger a binge or a binge-purge episode. The patient continues to record this information for the entire four months of treatment, which is the recommended length of therapy. I try to suggest ways to make it easier: The patient might make her notations at the time she is actually eating, as she may not remember what she ate when returning home at the end of the day; "stickum" notes are most helpful as they can be tucked away in a pocket and placed in the record directly. Also included in this first step is weighing oneself once a week. This is something some patients never do, whereas others weigh themselves many times a day; it is equally hard for both groups to adapt to this requirement.

If the patient keeps these records for at least six days of the first week, she then advances to the second step, which is to establish a regular eating pattern of three meals and three snacks per day. This does require some advanced planning, so that one does not get caught without food available when it is snacktime or meal time. No mention is made of what food the patient should eat; it doesn't matter whether a bowl of cereal or a cookie is eaten for breakfast. The effort here is to develop the habit of eating in the morning and not trying to save calories for the end of the day. This usually takes more than a week to accomplish, even though no specific menu or calorie intake needs to be achieved. I do suggest that the patient use snacktime to get in some of the five recommended servings of fruit or vegetables, pointing out how easy it is to keep a small bag of cut-up carrots, peppers, apple, or other fruit in one's purse or attaché to have handy at any time. Most patients are shocked that they are not gaining weight during this time. This interval is a good opportunity to explain that one decreases the incidence of bingeing as one eats more regularly. Advice is also provided on when and where to eat and on cooking and shopping. The following are some examples: sit and eat at a table in a room other than your bedroom; do not watch television while eating; put down your fork between mouthfuls; do not buy a lot of trigger foods; do not take more money to the store than you need; plan ahead what you will buy; carry a list and stick to it. It is helpful to have enough food at home of a kind you feel comfortable eating. Record keeping is continued in this second stage.

The next two areas of change work together, even though they are separated as step 3 and step 4. To help prevent bingeing, they can be started while working on step 2. These areas include planning ahead the activities you can do in place of bingeing and thinking of ways to prevent situations that might lead to a binge, all of which, it is hoped, can be foreseen with the help of the food records that are continued throughout treatment. Some examples are taking a bath, writing a letter, taking a walk, calling a friend, or writing in your diary. If the patient is at a family party or office picnic, she can read to the younger children, take them for a walk, or offer to help to clean up—anything to keep busy is important. These suggestions all sound good but are difficult to implement when your feelings take you elsewhere. It is not easily accomplished on the first try, so I, as the nurse, must encourage the patient to retry various ideas until she finds the ones that are helpful. This is also a time for her to take stock and see what behavioral changes, if any, have occurred. Has bingeing and purging been reduced or eliminated? If not, why? The timing of therapy or this particular program may not be right for this patient. At this point I may consult with staff to recommend additional or alternative help.

Step 5 in the program discusses why dieting is just a setup for failure. According to Dr. Fairburn there are three types of dieting: (1) not eating for long periods; (2) restricting the overall amount eaten; and (3) avoiding certain types of food. At this stage there is a discussion of why deprivation of food is a setup for a binge (191–92). Slowly introducing the idea of eating a small amount of anything one wants, and enjoying the taste is difficult but extremely important. The food records that are being kept throughout are helpful in picking and choosing the best times to do this, and choosing a safe place and safe company is of utmost importance.

Explaining the difference between a *lapse* and a *relapse* comes in the final stage, Step 6, of this self-help program. Most of us get discouraged when we slip back into an old habit, so it is important to tell oneself it was just a slip, that it's over, so now back to the new regime, rather than feeling, "I blew it, so I might as well forget everything I learned and worked so hard on for the last months." It is important to say: "I am human. I did something I am not happy about, but now it is back to my newly learned habits . . . immediately!" It is not helpful to wait until tomorrow or next week. This is part of having realistic expectations. Things are not always 100 percent. This program takes approximately sixteen weeks as people progress at different speeds and in different ways. Most find the program helpful and do change some aspect of their behavior. One must keep in mind that this program does not work for everyone; along the way the patient reviews what is happening. This may tell her that this program is not for her, that further and more intensive treatment is needed.

The nurse's role is one of encouragement and support. To be a good listener and not be judgmental is most important. Sometimes it is difficult not to get overly involved; the nurse must remember that her role is not to be a therapist but to stay focused on the topic. Very often people want to discuss various problems, but it is the nurse's task to get the conversation back to the food records and off, say, the movie they saw or why everyone at work seems to be against them. Everyone is different, and the nurse must be aware of the patient's individuality every time she enters the treatment room. Some people prefer the nurse to remain aloof, whereas others like that hug or extra smile when times are really tough, as well as when things are going well. In that way the work of repatterning takes place in a supportive atmosphere where the boundaries of exchange between nurse and patient provide a clear focus on behavior and attitude toward food and eating.

Reference

Fairburn, Christopher. 1995. *Overcoming Binge Eating*. New York: Guilford.

11

Individual Psychotherapy: A Long Journey of Growth and Change

INGE S. ORTMEYER

> Character cannot be developed in ease and quiet. Only through experience of trial and suffering can the soul be strengthened, vision cleared, ambition inspired, and success achieved.
>
> —Helen Keller

How does psychotherapy heal psychic pain and overcome disordered eating?

Some individuals, particularly late-adolescent and young-adult women whose eating disorders are transitory and maturational, often respond to short-term individual and group therapy. Others who have experienced difficulties in many areas of life for many years require more intensive lengthy psychotherapy. This involves duration of treatment from at least one to several years with a frequency of one or more sessions weekly. The continuity and intensity experienced by the person under such conditions facilitates recovery, change, and growth in a way that is less likely in the short-term treatment programs that have proliferated in recent years.

The early nineties have seen a transformation in the allocation and delivery of mental health services. This has significantly affected the way psychotherapists work. Insurance companies, which traditionally had reimbursed subscribers for a portion of the cost of psychotherapy, are increasingly restricting their coverage through the use of managed care organizations. Short-term cognitive and behavior modification programs offering symptom management have a large following and are favored by the managed health system. While many eating disordered patients respond to such programs, a significant number do not respond at all or relapse once they have completed the program. In such programs the emphasis on the eating disorder as a symptom to be overcome and the prescription of behavior overshadows exploration of the meaning of past and present experience and the relationship with the therapist, which are the cornerstones of psychodynamic or psychoanalytically oriented psychotherapy.

Many of the people I have worked with required and responded to approaches that were psychoanalytically informed but also addressed their symptoms. *Psychoanalytically informed* refers to a perspective focused on the "development and emergence of the patient's authentic, personal voice from the internalization of social forces and significant others" (Mitchell and Black 1995, 213–14). The therapist and patient engage in an exploration and analysis of the patient's experiences, past and present, with particular attention to repetitive themes in relationships and behavior, which are often reenacted in the therapeutic encounter. In the course of the work, the patient both cognitively reflects on and emotionally reacts to previously unformulated experience. The accrued insight is believed to lead to self-awareness and change in the person's character, behavior, and relationships. With due regard for the value of techniques and a knowledge base, let me underscore that relationships, not techniques, heal. What is curative is the therapist offering some form of basic parental responsiveness that was missed early on.

Both the process and the goals of cognitive-behavioral treatment (CBT) are different from psychodynamic psychotherapy. In CBT the therapist is directive and didactic, even at times authoritative, with the goal of stopping the symptoms, be they restricted eating or binge-purging, by changing the thoughts, beliefs, feelings, and pattern of action that maintain them. Outcome studies have demonstrated the efficacy of CBT for many patients, but not for those who suffer from significant and enduring interpersonal and personality difficulties.

Such patients lack the integration and capacity for self-regulation essential to engage constructively in CBT. Bruce Arnow recommends "combining and sequencing cognitive-behavioral treatment with dynamic therapy, rather than attempting to integrate these treatments seamlessly (1996, 137–38). I have found that they can be integrated if both approaches are modified in accordance with the patient's capacity to respond. Kathryn Zerbe (1993) notes that at least one-third of eating disordered patients do not recover despite cognitive, psychoeducational, behavioral, and psychopharmacologic therapies. She believes that "psychotherapeutic—especially psychodynamic—therapy must be integrated with other treatment modalities to provide patients with the best chance of full recovery" (15–16).

I find Harry Stack Sullivan's detailed inquiry (1954) very useful in engaging the patient in a functional analysis of the disordered eating, including the concomitant obsessions and rituals. The inquiry is conducted in an empathic way and encompasses the journalistic questions of who, what, when, where, how, and why of the patient's experience. The frequency of the bingeing and purging, what is eaten and how it is purged, accompanying thoughts and feelings, and the nature of the purging and the aftermath are explored. Whether the person is aware of precipitating experiences or triggers needs to be determined. An inquiry is made about the person's weight history and body image, and about family members' weight history and their concerns about weight and dieting. At the same time, notice is taken of exceptions and inconsistencies, calling attention to islands of health or times when the patient is not thinking about weight, shape, and food, or is not engaged in eating or purging. The detailed inquiry includes interest in positive, normal, and healthy aspects of her life. The groundwork is thus laid for the subsequent therapeutic work in recovering and restoring a healthier self.

If the person has not been in treatment before, we discuss the therapeutic process, emphasizing the collaboration and the mutuality of the work. Even if the person has had previous treatment, I talk about the symptoms and obsession as an expression of feelings and states of being. I will often say, "This is not about eating and weight, it's about using your body to enact and express your feelings." In effect, many eating disordered patients have to be walked through the treatment process. I also say that over the course of treatment, patients may be overwhelmed by their feelings and may experience a worsening of their symptoms.

Recently more attention has been given to dissociative (Jones 1991) features and conditions in patients with eating disorders. Of particular interest to me is Alexithymia (McDougall 1991; Swiller 1988) as a prominent feature. Alexithymia is a cognitive/affective pattern characterized by an inability to identify and differentiate emotions, concrete thinking, and an impoverished symbolic and fantasy life. Feelings are not experienced at all or are experienced as global states such as dysphoria, an anxious, uneasy state without specificity. The ability to identify and put words to, or label, feelings has not developed. Often the unidentified feelings are projected onto the body and are transformed into obsessions about the body and ritualistic eating. In working with this phenomenon, I engage the patient in exploring her underlying feelings, picking up the threads of the experience generating the feelings, and then I draw the connection to how this is expressed in her body, her eating behavior, and her thoughts. This process of helping the patient experience her feelings and think about what is happening is a crucial aspect of the treatment.

It is widely held that, although anorexia nervosa and bulimia are distinct diagnostic entities, considerable overlap, as well as differences, exists in their features and dynamics. In recent years, so many of the patients I see have both anorexic and bulimic characteristics that I'm often hard pressed to make the differential diagnosis, particularly when they are at a low weight. Actually the percentage of pure restricting anorexics with no bulimic symptoms or behavior—as discussed by Levenkron (1978) and Bruch (1978)—has remained fairly constant over the years and is small compared to the heterogeneous group of bulimics.

THE THERAPEUTIC PROCESS

As a female therapist who has treated mostly women with eating disorders, my discussion is based on that experience with certain gender-related reference points. It is not my intention to slight males suffering from eating disorders or male therapists. Clearly nurturing and empathy are not the exclusive domain of female therapists. Although some of the observations and discussion here are applicable to males suffering from eating disorders, who comprise 5 to 10 percent of sufferers, significant differences exist in the psychological issues.

The therapist treating the restricting anorexic should proceed slowly and gingerly with respect to the person's need to preserve her boundaries and guard against intrusiveness. Here, the challenge is to engage her in a therapeutic alliance without falling into the transference traps of overprotectiveness, overattentiveness, overconcern, and control. The patient will do her best, without intention or awareness, to reenact with the therapist her relationship with parental figures and important others. The therapist may have powerful needs to nurture and rescue that undermine her effectiveness as a therapist. It is important to avoid replicating the struggle over eating and gaining weight in which the patient engages with her family. In contrast to the restricting anorexic, restricting and normal-weight bulimics generally welcome the therapist's involvement, which includes more active inquiry and exploration.

In my work with this challenging and difficult group of patients, I have found it vital to collaborate with a physician and nutritionist who are knowledgeable about eating disorders and the psychological issues involved. It is helpful for the physician to set the contract regarding a threshold weight, thus freeing the therapist to address the patient's terrors about eating and gaining weight. For many eating disordered individuals, ongoing work with a nutritionist or dietitian specializing in eating disorders is a vital adjunct to psychotherapy. The nutritionist can be more directive and can monitor the patient's eating and weight, while the therapist can address the patient's fears and dynamic issues.

A critical issue for eating disordered patients is body-image distortion and the "relentless pursuit of thinness," as Hilde Bruch (1978) described it. An important prognostic and diagnostic sign is the patient's response over time to the question of whether she would be willing to gain some weight, (e.g., 5 to 10 pounds) as the price of recovery. Many clinicians believe that the rigid and ongoing adherence to an unrealistic weight portends chronicity (Johnson and Connors 1987).

The middle phase of treatment involves the further exploration of the person's experience and feelings underlying the anorexic or bulimic behavior. We move into detailed discussion of how she sees the therapist and what images and illusions she brings to the therapeutic relationship. In contrast to traditional psychoanalysis, interpretation of the transference in terms of parental figures is selective with bulimics and may be contraindicated as too intrusive with anorexics. Johnson (1991) generalizes that restricting anorexics have experienced maternal overinvolvement, whereas bulimics have experienced maternal under-involvement. He goes on to recommend that therapists provide a corrective experience in their interaction with the patient.

I have found that, in contrast to my work with noneating disordered patients, my countertransference is more intense with eating disordered patients and can be overwhelming. Therapists differ in their definition of countertransference. For me, countertransference is the sum total of all my reactions to the patient and our work, including unconscious associations and fantasies as well as reactions and feelings of which I am aware. The unconscious components come into awareness when I note and then analyze an action or comment on my part, which is unusual. I believe that the ongoing interplay between the transference and countertransference as described above is the most vital aspect of the therapeutic work.

Many patients with eating disorders have great difficulty tolerating and modulating their intense neediness and bad feelings, particularly as they give up their symptoms. This is enacted in the therapeutic relationship by either demanding relief or dismissing the therapist as useless. It is at this juncture that I may find myself feeling exhausted, frustrated, thwarted, impotent, useless, and sometimes confused. Although undoubtedly some of my own personal issues contribute to these feelings, a good portion are in response to patients' projections of their intolerable feelings. Epstein (1987) refers to this phenomenon as the "bad-analyst-feeling." It certainly gives me a sense of what the patient is experiencing when I analyze and process the countertransference.

Sharing my reactions with other female therapists has been particularly helpful to me. Among the countertransference issues we hold in common are our own sensitivity to cultural pressures to diet and to be thin, as well as our feelings about our own bodies. The therapist's weight and shape, as well as changes in these characteristics, are invariably noted by eating disordered individuals. Whether the female therapist is thin, average, or heavy, her patients will react. Discussion of these reactions and accessible fantasies may be productive in terms of repetitive themes of body-image distortion, competition, envy, and disparagement. I have noted that as I entered middle age, patients became less attentive to my shape. Therapists who harbor their unresolved issues about beauty and shape may experience envy and competitive feelings with patients who are more attractive. Male therapists are also undoubtedly affected by issues of physical attractiveness and shape to which they must be attentive.

Deficits in self-regulating and self-soothing capacities are characteristic of most of the eating disordered women I have worked with. The causes for these deficits are so varied and complex as to defy generalization. However, they include constitution, health, early trauma, and derailment or detours in their emotional development. These deficits are manifested in the person's inability to deal with frustration, unpleasant affects, and distressing experiences. Connections are broken and reactions are short-circuited by automatically turning to or away from food and becoming obsessed about weight and shape. Developing the capacity to bear feelings and modulate affect involves both specific and general strategies. These include using a journal and exploring ways of stimulating, expressing, satisfying, and comforting oneself other than eating or purging. Further, the person needs to be encouraged to turn to people and relationships, rather than their bodies and food, to meet their needs. *A guiding principle that I articulate is that the eating disorder is a solution, however misguided, that has meaning and value for the individual.* The therapeutic alliance and work promotes the individual's development of her capacity for self-reflection, her sensitivity to personal needs, and her empathy for the needs and feelings of others. Over the course of more lengthy and intensive therapy, the work and therapeutic relationship is taken in and woven into the patient's personality.

Case Discussion

To illustrate, I will describe my work over a period of six years with Laura, a twenty-five-year-old woman who is bulimic. Her issues included body-image distortion, alcoholism, depression, learning disabilities, and the possibility of earlier sexual abuse. Medication, hospitalization, nutritional consultation, and family and group therapy supported intensive psychotherapy when they were indicated.

I saw Laura twice a week for the greater part of six years and once a week as we moved toward termination. Her physician referred her to me. She had previously seen another therapist for some months during which she "lied her brains out." The presenting problems were depression, daily purging and preoccupation with her weight, and lack of direction in her life. She had taken a medical leave from a fashion college she was attending. When first seen, Laura looked attractive, of medium height, and slender, with curly brown hair framing her girlish expressive face. She was dressed casually in an individualistic yet preppy style. Her emblem was a dark streak running down the side of her hair. She was nervous and tearful, referring to how lost she felt. She was most upset about dropping out of school. She had been overwhelmed there almost from the beginning, unable to concentrate and work. She became increasingly obsessed with her weight and felt driven to throw up even after normal eating.

Laura's bulimic symptoms had begun the previous year, her senior year in high school. She had moved with her family from California to the East the previous year. The move had been, and still was, emotionally painful for her. She particularly missed her boyfriend and best girlfriend. While she made a few new female and male friends, she saw herself as an outsider. She felt she had to fake a cheerfulness and confidence that were totally at odds with her true feelings. She had also gained about thirty pounds and was very upset at her weight of 160 pounds. Her father had teased her saying she looked like a "red barn" and had also remarked that Laura's mother looked as if she were "eight months pregnant." Her father had been overweight, but had lost weight ten years ago and remains slender. Laura was able to lose the weight with strenuous dieting, and she went down to 110 pounds. She believed the only way to avoid weight gain was to restrict her eating severely. And she found in bulimia the solution to the unbearable tension between her emotional and physical hunger and her terror of gaining weight. Her pattern of restricted eating became punctuated by binges followed by vomiting. Upon leaving school, she had moved back into her parents' home.

Laura's father, a lawyer, was described as quiet, reserved, and absorbed in his business, his computer, and his projects. Her mother, a homemaker, was characterized as demanding and critical of Laura, unhappy, socially inactive, and a heavy drinker. One sibling, a married brother ten years older, lived several hours away. I met with Laura and her parents on a few occasions during the initial phase of our work. They impressed me as reserved but responsive people, who were obviously concerned and perplexed by Laura. Both parents came from deprived and depriving backgrounds. They had overcome the adversity of their earlier lives by dint of their ability, hard work, and sheer will. There was a history of alcoholism in her mother's family that figured significantly in the physical abuse her mother had endured. Several members of Laura's extended family had committed suicide. Laura was deeply affected by the death of a favorite uncle the week she started to see me.

Laura's experience with death in her extended family and her exposure to suicide as an option when life becomes unbearable was reinforced by the suicide of her good friend during the Christmas holidays. Laura had been devastated and had continued to feel guilty that she hadn't done more to help her friend. Having known three people who killed themselves, she found herself wishing she were dead when she felt really bad, as she did when she left school. Since Laura's depression lifted somewhat over the early months of treatment, I did not refer her for a medication consultation at that point, but I did so later. Her vulnerability to agitated depression has been a theme throughout our work, even when she was on medication. In time, she found code words to describe these states: "The blue meanies are coming," "I'm having UMS" (ugly mood swings), "I'm on the pity pot," or "I want to throw myself in the garbage pail like a piece of trash." She also found code words to describe her body in order to express her feelings; "My body feels like a space suit." The ability to use language rather than symptoms and self-destructive behavior to express her feelings was a major step in her developing a more integrated self and ultimately recovering.

Laura described her childhood as very unhappy. Her mother was demanding and critical of her but never clear about what she expected from Laura. When Laura was a child, her mother frequently hit her for such infractions as spilling milk, getting dirty, or messing up the house. Her mother also often yelled and made cruel statements about how Laura couldn't do anything right and caused too much trouble. She would also yell at Laura's father and brother, and Laura recalled bitter altercations between her brother and mother when her brother was an adolescent. In contrast to Laura, her brother rebelled and fought back. Father would both physically and emotionally detach and lose himself in his work or projects at home. Laura remembered that she felt confused about why she was unable to please her mother. An early memory is of wanting to walk to school alone on her first day. In our work, she understood this as an example of how she dealt with separation, anxiety, and neediness by isolating herself. As she grew older, Laura wished her mother could simply tell her she was having a bad day and couldn't control herself. In a dream Laura reported early in our work, her mother took her to have her wrist cut off. An electric saw went zip and cut off her wrist. It was very painful. She was crying and thinking about her mother making the doctor cut off her wrist. By association, she thought of going to the dentist for painful treatment and being punished for her bulimia. In response, I said that I wondered if she felt this treatment would be worse than the illness. Over the course of our work, as both Laura and her parents changed, her anger and largely negative view of them shifted to a more balanced realistic perspective.

Although Laura was able to talk openly and in detail about her family, her losses, and her feelings, she was embarrassed and circumspect in talking about sex, alcohol and eating. She was particularly embarrassed to talk about her body, referring to her breasts as her chest, and was unable to utter the words for sexual organs. Her first period occurred on the family boat when she was about ten or eleven. She was mortified, tried to hide the stained underwear, and believed that God was punishing her. Her severe repression and anxiety bespoke of possible childhood traumatic sexual experience and/or extreme guilt about sexual exploration and masturbation. Annie Fursland (1987) links women's eating and sexual desire as sources of shame and torment. Laura has not been able to recover any memories of sexual abuse.

During the early months of our work, she spoke about drinking in high school but denied excessive drinking since starting treatment. She was most guarded in revealing the details of her eating patterns and purging. She was a vegetarian who limited her diet to a few foods she felt she could handle. She would vomit whenever she felt she ate too much, often after eating an amount that would be normal for most people. Early in treatment, she acknowledged that her vomiting was as much a response to her emotional state as it was to what and how much she had eaten. Body-image distortion, preoccupation with weight, and terror of becoming fat were prominent early in treatment and continued to persist throughout, gradually lessening in intensity as she progressed in her recovery.

A significant feature in her presentation was her tendency to become confused and blocked in her ability to think when she was anxious. This confusion and blocking was noted to some extent in every one of our sessions for years. Her difficulty in thinking could be attributed to her Alexithymia (McDougall 1991) but also suggested cognitive difficulties in processing information and her thoughts. Exploration of her school history revealed that, although she had learned little, she had managed to pass because she was quiet, compliant, and well-behaved. She could read mechanically but had little comprehension and recall of what she had read. Her fund of information was very limited. She was surprised that she was promoted from grade to grade and even graduated from high school given her marginal performance. The first summer I saw Laura, she enrolled in a college-level course to see if she could handle college. She was anxious and overwhelmed to the point that she could not follow the instructor's lecture or comprehend the textbook. Although I felt that other factors were operating—such as her drinking, anxiety, and depression—I suspected significant learning disabilities and referred her for a psychoeducational evaluation. The evaluation found significant weaknesses in auditory-processing skills, reading comprehension, word retrieval, knowledge of linguistic rules, study skills, and general fund of knowledge. She followed the recommendations of the evaluator and enrolled in remedial college courses, which she was able to complete successfully. Her initial reaction to this information about her learning difficulties was to feel that her sense of worthlessness and hopelessness about her future was confirmed. Her relentless pursuit of thinness gave her the illusion of control by projecting onto her body her sense of defectiveness and the attempt to establish control. It took her a long time to accept a positive framing of her difficulties and to try the recommended strategies to compensate for her specific learning disabilities.

From the beginning I was concerned about Laura's drinking. While she complained bitterly about her mother's drinking and its destructive impact on the family, she denied her own drinking problem and resisted all attempts on my part to engage her in addressing it. After several months she had a blackout experience, which frightened her and broke her denial. She stopped drinking and began attending Alcoholics Anonymous meetings daily. While her sobriety represented growth, Laura had great difficulty dealing with some of the consequences. These included the loss involved in relinquishing friendships that had been based on alcohol, the consequent isolation and loneliness, and the experience of being overwhelmed by painful feelings. Over some months, her bulimia and depression worsened to the point where she felt out of control and suicidal. She agreed to admit herself to a hospital, where she remained for six months. During this time she and her family became involved in family therapy at the hospital, and she became involved in group therapy. Although I had met with Laura and her family periodically, both she and her family had refused ongoing work. She worked with another therapist while she was hospitalized and resumed therapy with me upon her discharge. She also participated with her family in family therapy with another therapist and joined a therapy group.

My work with Laura combined a psychodynamic relational approach with active cognitive-behavioral interventions later in the treatment when she was more capable of tolerating stress and anticipating and delaying her own reactions. I used the first year to introduce Laura to the process of therapy and our mutual participation, my interest in her candid response to me, and anticipation of her discomfort during the course of therapy. Her alcoholism and learning disabilities were explored and attended to in addition to her eating disorder, dysphoria, and anxiety. Dynamically and developmentally, Laura had a fragmented, unevolved sense of herself. She lacked the inner resources to modulate her anxiety and to soothe

and regulate herself. Her self-image was of someone who was difficult, troublesome, and incompetent. She had also internalized the
family's sexual repression and could not countenance sexual exploration either alone or with a partner. As noted by Zerbe (1995),
shame, inhibition of joy and liveliness, spiritual malaise, and trauma
were significant factors in shutting down her sexuality. The only
exceptions to her sexual abstinence had taken place under the influence of alcohol. While she had developed superficial social skills,
she had been thwarted in her attempts to reach out to others for
understanding, care, and intimacy. A combination of her experience
in therapy and increased ability to communicate and engage in relationships gradually enabled her frozen sexuality to thaw.

In the early therapeutic relationship, Laura expected me to
ignore, misunderstand, criticize, and reject her. A premature attempt
to help her with symptom management failed dismally; it only
heightened her sense of failure and chaos. She needed an empathic
holding environment in which she could express her neediness, her
bad feelings, her shame, as well as her creativity, humor, and idio-
syncrasies. As our relationship deepened following her hospitalization, Laura moved into an idealizing transference in which she
expected me to be perfectly attuned and understanding of her. Not
being a perfect therapist, and subject to countertransference reactions, there were times when I talked too much or too little, was
insensitive, and misunderstood her. In turn, she experienced familiar reactions of withdrawing and turning on herself. There were times
when the depth of her hopeless and helpless despair numbed me.
In response to prolonged confusion and blanking out on Laura's
part, I would become distracted and lose the connection with her. I
would then jolt myself into pressing her to respond. I used my countertransferential responses to guess at what she might be experiencing. She was gradually able to tell me when certain inquiries or
subjects made her so anxious she couldn't think or when I talked
too much or too little or didn't understand her. Multiple repetitions
of this process contributed to her sense of effectiveness and were
empowering. For more than three years of our work together, Laura
was on antidepressant medication. While it alleviated her depression somewhat, it had little effect on her anxiety. I was struck by a
curious dissociation from her depression while on medication, in

contrast to her being engulfed by it before she started the medication. Her bulimia has waxed and waned over the course of our work.

In the later years she was able to use behavioral strategies with success and was also able to turn to people in her life other than me for involvement. When she became overwhelmed by the vicissitudes of life, she still sought relief in the bulimic cycle. This occurred following the breakup of her first intimate relationship with a man. She attended college where she experienced success in her courses and satisfaction in her social life.

At a time when lengthy psychoanalytic psychotherapy is on the wane, Laura stands out as a person in whom the complex interplay of issues required very intensive work *over time* to enable her to evolve and realize her potential as a competent and integrated person.

References

Arnow, Bruce. 1996. "Cognitive-Behavioral Therapy for Bulimia Nervosa." In Joellen Werne, ed., *Treating Eating Disorders*, 101–42. San Francisco: Jossey-Bass.

Bruch, Hilde. 1978. *The Golden Cage: The Enigma of Anorexia Nervosa*. Cambridge, Mass.: Harvard University Press.

Epstein, Lawrence. 1987. "The Problem of the Bad-Analyst-Feeling." *Modern Psychoanalysis* 12:35–45.

Fursland, Annie. 1987. "Eve was Framed: Food and Sex and Women's' Shame." In Lawrence Marilyn, ed., *Fed Up and Hungry*. New York: Bedrick Books.

Johnson, Craig. 1991. "Treatment of Eating-Disordered Patients with Borderline and False-Self/Narcissistic Disorders." In Craig Johnson, ed., *Psychodynamic Treatment of Anorexia Nervosa and Bulimia*. New York: Guilford.

Johnson, C., and M. E. Connors. 1987. *The Etiology and Treatment of Bulimia Nervosa*. New York: Basic Books.

Jones, Dorothy. 1991. "Alexithymia: Inner Speech and Linkage Impairment." *Clinical Social Work Journal* 19:237–49.

Levenkron, Steven. 1978. *Best Little Girl in the World*. Chicago, Ill: Contemporary Books (Warner Paperback).

McDougall, Joyce. 1991. *Theaters of the Mind*, 147–79. New York: Brunner/Mazel.

Mitchell, Stephen A., and Margaret J. Black. 1995. *Freud and Beyond.* New York: Basic Books,

Sullivan, H. H. 1954. *The Psychiatric Interview.* New York: Norton.

Swiller, Hillel. 1998. "Alexithymia: Treatment Utilizing Combined Individual and Group Psychotherapy." *International Journal of Group Psychotherapy* 38:47–61

Zerbe, Kathryn J. 1993. *The Body Betrayed.* Washington D.C.: American Psychiatric Press.

———. 1995. "The Emerging Sexual Self of the Patient with an Eating Disorder: Implications for Treatment." *Eating Disorders: The Journal of Treatment and Prevention* 3, no. 3 (fall): 197–215.

12

Young Adult Women: Reflections on Recurring Themes and a Discussion of the Treatment Process and Setting

NANCY KING

As a psychotherapist who specializes in the treatment of eating disorders, I see many women of college age, as well as recent college graduates. Certain themes recur in varying degrees and disguises. They appear in my weekly groups as well as in my individual sessions with these young women. Though the causation of eating disorders is considered to be multifaceted, including genetic predispositions and physiological components, the therapist, in session, addresses the content that emerges both verbally and interactively.

A devastating and confusing mix of societal messages continues to surface and present in treatment as young women battle the demands of the nineties—the "Superwoman Syndrome." As they look to their futures, young women feel driven to have all and be all—and in so doing they must deal with the realities of competing with Mom, Dad, husband/lover, and peers—both male and female. Some are terrified; some are energized. Some want to attempt to meet the challenge head on; some want to flee from it. Trying to be a superwoman requires working toward goals nearly impossible to attain. The mass media has promoted an image of the woman who is able to "do it all"—be the perfect lover, mother, and career performer. The operative word here is *perfect*. To get it right for a young woman suffering from an eating disorder, it *all* has to be perfect. As though this were not impossible enough, coupled with being "competent, sexy, and nurturant," she must be thin (Gordon 1989, 47). The complete extraordinary package includes thinness, as that, I believe, exhibits the ultimate control. "Bulimic [and I would add anorexic] women present an exaggerated picture of what has become a common dilemma among contemporary female college students: that of integrating values of achievement and mastery with an underlying self-concept that is defined in terms of nurturance, physical attractiveness, and an entwinement of one's own identity with relationship to others" (Gordon 1989, 46). Many of today's young women are in conflict: on the one hand trying to be a hard-working achiever, which often includes being competitive—sometimes with men; on the other hand, feeling the pull toward the older, more traditional role of the female—subservient and care-taking with regard to men and family. To deal with both sides of this conflict as she strives to get it all perfect, the eating disorder becomes the coping mechanism. Whereas Jones (1985) refers to the personality organization of the bulimic as the "false-self," I choose to broaden the concept to include the anorexic young woman as well. Further, I liken the personality of a young woman suffering from an eating disorder to the image of a chameleon—one who changes her colors to suit the circumstance of the moment—to fit in at all costs—*to blend*. It is the work of the therapist and individual together to find the one *true* color—the one that can ultimately be worn with ease at all times, in all circumstances: the "color" of the person within.

Many of our patients have been conditioned by well-intentioned parents to believe that achievement and success in college—and in life in general—is what life is all about. To achieve and to succeed in today's competitive world is no simple task. Because pleasing parents is often paramount, these young women may find themselves pursuing Mother's unfulfilled dreams or substituting for Father's unborn son. A different conflict may surface for some young women: "How can I possibly surpass Mom? I'd feel so guilty!" Dickstein (1989) states, "The consequent frustration of denying their own, possibly different, work, career and life-style goals can lead very directly to swallowing anger along with food and then relieving resultant anxiety, anger, and other personal problems by purging" (114). A patient once said to me, "I'm so angry all the time; the only respectable way I know to get rid of it is through the purge!" This occurred about six months into her treatment with me. Since at the onset of her treatment she was totally unaware of the rage within herself, I viewed this as progress. Of course her future work continued to be the excruciating and arduous task of being angry directly with the appropriate sources, rather than with herself, and finding a constructive resolution of that anger.

For these women caught up in this superwoman syndrome, thinness equals perfection. It also represents being in control. "If I have my thinness, I can cope," say these women. "When all else goes awry, when I feel confused and unable to deal with things around me, I can *look* perfect; that is my protection; my suit of armor." And that is what it becomes—that is what protects and eventually isolates these often lonely young women from life and living. When an individual measures her self-worth by the numbers on a scale, it becomes "thin at any price"—and the price can be very high—the cost of her life.

An added feminist perspective to this country's worship of thinness in women cannot be overlooked and, I believe, must be seriously considered. In *The Beauty Myth*, Naomi Wolf (1991) talks about the very theme I see in my practice: successful, young women obsessed with thinness. "America, which has the greatest number of women who have made it into the male sphere, also leads the world with female anorexia" (181). Wolf connects the onset of the increase in women's preoccupation with their weight with their attainment of the right to vote, received in 1920. And the obsession increased. The flapper image of the late twenties into the thirties further illustrates this point, with the flattened breasts and curveless clothes. In the fifties women were given a reprieve as domesticity was "in," and the fuller figure was reaccepted. But in the mid-sixties Twiggy became the role model of many women—a prepubescent tubular body, which appeared to have the fragility of a twig that might snap in the wind. Wolf says, "When women came en masse into *male spheres*, that pleasure had to be overridden by an urgent social expedient that would make women's bodies into the prisons that their homes no longer were" (184). Are women trying to be less feminine in their attempts to compete in a male-dominant society? Perhaps it is but a different version of the chameleon of which I spoke earlier.

Wolf (1991) talks exquisitely of her "One Stone Solution" (186). One stone, the British measurement of fourteen pounds, is the average amount of weight women aspire to lose—a weight that will have 50 percent of dieting women well below their ideal weight that is natural and beautiful to their bodies. But society set it up that way— and women bought it. Without the extra thin body, a woman is not truly successful. And as she struggles to attain and maintain it, like quicksilver, she cannot hold onto it because physically she is crying out for the sustenance she needs. Her mind and body are in conflict. She is unable to be as successful as she might be in whatever endeavor she undertakes.

Wolf cites research by S. C. Wooley and O. W. Wooley which illustrated that preoccupations with weight lead to "a virtual collapse of self-esteem and sense of effectiveness," while J. Polivy and C. P. Herman found that "prolonged and periodic caloric restriction resulted in a distinctive personality whose traits are *passivity, anxiety,* and *emotionality*" (Wolf 1991, 187, 188). Thus Wolf concludes, "It is those traits, and not thinness for its own sake, that the dominant culture wants to create in the private sense of self of recently liberated women, in order to cancel out the dangers of their liberation" (188).

As a therapist today working with these young women, I believe that Wolf makes a cogent argument, one we cannot ignore. In their relentless pursuit of thinness, many of these young women are nowhere nearly as effective in their overall performance as they have the capacity to be—were they not suffering from the often crippling effects of their self-imposed starvation or their binge-purge obsession.

I try to be aware of the complexities of the eating disorders as we know them. I believe it is essential for people working with individuals suffering from eating disorders to have worked through their own issues regarding body image, weight, and food. Our astute awareness of countertransferential material is essential. For example, if a patient says to a therapist, "It may be okay for *you* to be five pounds overweight, but it is not okay for *me*," the therapist, ideally, must react to the patient's distress, and not her own. If, as a therapist, I get caught up in my *patient's* innuendo, I cannot be as effective in understanding and exploring her own desperation as I would want to be.

I work in a style that can best be described as eclectic with a psychodynamic base. I will try almost anything within professional parameters to foster a safe, nonthreatening arena in which an individual and I can explore together the depths of the suffering—or oftentimes break through the defenses and denial in order to first acknowledge the suffering. I present myself as three-dimensional. I gingerly let out a little of me over time, becoming more human and less of a blank slate. I am considerably active in my work, believing that engaging the individual early on is essential to a good therapeutic fit. Because many of the people whom I see are so rigidly one-dimensional—though they can *play* at being many roles, like the chameleon—I must provide them with a nurturing womb in which to grow as they attempt to risk being more real. I laugh with them, and I even poke fun at my own obsessionalism at times. Then, ideally, they can begin to take themselves less seriously.

Trust in *all* therapeutic settings is essential. In this population trust is a prerequisite to getting work done. Usually, in order to trust someone, a person must first feel safe and relatively comfortable. As therapists, I believe we have to make this happen for these people because they come in, for the most part, so guarded against their own feelings *and* so defended! They are terrified that I am going to make them give up their lifeline (i.e., symptoms)—and, let's face it, I am going to do just that if I am successful.

As the therapeutic relationship strengthens, so does the work progress. The womb mentioned earlier need not be totally nurturing; in fact, it must eventually allow for optimal frustration in the treatment process (Lonergan 1992). A patient, Ann, told me that she had been struggling for two weeks with whether to tell me that she was angry with me. She was bothered by having learned that I was treating a student at her college whom she did not like very much. As we talked, I learned that this person was not a close friend of Ann's but that she *was* a "snobby, skinny dancer." We talked about Ann's jealousy of both the other student's thinness *and* Ann's having to "share" me with her. Ann was frustrated when it became apparent that I was not going to stop seeing the other student. We talked about this and her fears and fantasies encompassing the situation. She was able to tell me that she had actually considered not seeing me anymore. Both Ann's frustration and conflict were apparent. These provided rich material in the treatment process and, in time, allowed Ann to grow in her ability to tolerate and express her emotions more readily. Conflict is essential for progress. Once an individual feels safe enough, she must be able to tolerate, experience, and explore the conflicts she acknowledges within herself. These conflicts may in fact make her at odds with what appears to be an unfair world; equally important, she may find herself at odds with her therapist. Because anger and conflict are usually so terrifying to our patients, they need support and encouragement to allow themselves to express these emotions and to tolerate them.

I allow patients to talk about their fear, helplessness, and sense of entrapment—all tied up in their symptom. I listen for their desperation and acknowledge it. But I do not try to fix it, and cannot of course—except in helping them to eventually fix it themselves. This acknowledgment allows the treatment to take root. Their symptom is their best friend and worst enemy simultaneously. I allow them to talk about it. I tolerate the often ghastly and graphic descriptions of their symptomatic behavior. This can be difficult for both patient and therapist, but it is truly a test for patients to *know* that they are understood and safe!

As treatment progresses, I consistently weave the connecting threads of symptoms to feelings. Eventually patients begin to do this for themselves. This is an exciting juncture in the treatment process and is mutually acknowledged.

Recovery usually includes the vital concept of mourning the loss of the symptom. First, we acknowledge together the realization that the symptom is not working as well as it used to. Next, we acknowledge together the symptom's absence entirely. Therapist and patient are *totally in tandem* during this process. I must overtly acknowledge the loss and fears of not having one's "best friend" anymore as a way of coping with life. My patients are both terrified and sad. I let them know that I know this, but I cannot take away the pain and frustration. I encourage discussion about the loss and the feelings that are rapidly surfacing. Mourning often includes the young woman's singing the praises of the "deceased." This is part of the recovery process. I listen. Usually, directly following this stage comes the terror of, "What do I now, 'without the deceased' " (i.e., the symptom)? Keeping in character with this metaphor, the individual may need to resurrect the "deceased" from time to time and become symptomatic. When the symptom is rendered powerless by the patient, another level of mourning via understanding is reached, usually accompanied by greater sadness, deeper fear, and often great anxiety. Finally the patient realizes that the notion "If I'm thin, it will all come together" is the ultimate myth that must be put to rest. Truth, as only truth can be for each individual, must evolve in its stead.

Because eating disorders are so pervasive, acknowledging any single success along the way is essential in the treatment process. Furthermore, negatives serve no purpose, as these individuals have, for the most part, negated themselves with their own self-scorn and hatred far beyond what the therapist will ever fully know. For these reasons, wherever possible, I eliminate the negative implications that arise in the treatment environment and am careful to avoid negative verbal constructs. One does not take steps *backward*; one may make a *lateral* move. One does not have a *slip*; one has an *episode*. And because one cannot undo what one has already accomplished, one is never "*back to square one.*" If ever the concept to "accentuate the positive, and eliminate the negative" were to apply, it is in the treatment of eating disorders.

There is no one exact way to treat or view individuals. I find that we therapists only get into trouble when we generalize. I am annoyed when I hear professionals talking about "eating-disordered women," as though they were Stepford Wives—all branded, doomed, and alike. I do not assume anything! A college student once came into my office and announced, "Today, I *feel* like an eating disorder." That's when I feigned ignorance—I didn't get it. I gently teased from her exactly what those words meant to *her* on that particular day. So the work began. As her description unfolded, so did her feelings. Gradually I became smarter, and we *both* got to know her better; then we began together to "get it." We were connected.

In addition to my function as an individual psychotherapist at the Wilkins Center, I also am a leader of three groups. Wilkins provides psychotherapy groups for adolescent girls, young women of college through postgraduate school age, adult moms with eating disorders, parent groups, and groups for women who suffer from compulsive overeating. Female young adults comprise one of my groups, which is the age group I have focused on in this writing. Most of the issues and facets of the treatment process discussed above are elements that appear on some level in the group setting. I see group therapy as a springboard to individual treatment, and vice versa. Issues often come up in one arena to be further explored in the other. The two modalities dovetail to enrich or facilitate the overall treatment process. Painful though it may be, the group offers young women who suffer from eating disorders a place to explore their issues among those who have found the same way of coping.

Group members learn to relate to one another as they may never have dared before—always being encouraged to come out from behind their masks, to cease changing colors, to be more and more real, and to continue to try to find their truest and most comfortable hue.

In addition to attempting the nearly impossible—that of being real—individuals in a group setting can eventually begin to exchange with peers painful, significant parts of their lives and emotions they may never have discussed with anyone other than the individual therapist. For today's young women, these experiences include not only the conflicts and pressures of the "Superwoman Syndrome," as described earlier, but also discussions around incidents of date rape and sexual abuse, topics that until recently have been taboo. The publicity surrounding these two subjects has encouraged women to come forward and discuss secrets formerly kept buried. For women with eating disorders, secrets that may have been pushed down with food and released only through the purge, or those kept hidden through the controlled parameters of anorexic behavior, can now be explored with peers in a safe arena.

As the group evolves, it is seen both as a microcosm of the real world (people relating to people) *and* as one's family, with certain group members taking on the roles of specific family members. People learn to identify their feelings, as situations within the group parallel circumstances within their own families. As the therapist vigilantly oversees the group's interactions, members are encouraged to express, allow, and tolerate anger—and to see that it does not destroy. Optimal frustration, as discussed earlier, will be experienced within a group setting, as well as in the individual setting, in order for the group to progress (Lonergan 1992).

Young women have psychically chosen eating disorders as their coping mechanisms for as many reasons as there are patients. The group setting helps individuals to flush out their hidden fears, conflicts, and frustrations. What is startling to me is the answer I most often hear to my rather simple question, "What do *you* want?" The answer is "I don't know, and anyway why does *that* matter?" No wonder these young women are angry—though they do not yet know it.

Hilde Bruch (1982) once said that one's ability to pursue goals in life on the basis of being *"worthwhile,* rather than *extraordinary"* might be a major indicator of recovery from an eating disorder. I support this concept. Relinquishing one's stranglehold on perfectionism allows for the growth necessary toward recovery.

Barbara Kinoy addresses prognosis for recovery in her preface to this book. She lists significant factors as reported in a study of recovered anorexic patients: personality strength, self-confidence, being ready, and being understood. From a therapist's perspective, I might cautiously embellish this list with the following: finding the courage to allow oneself to be who she truly discovers herself to be—when she is no longer a chameleon who changes "hue" to suit each situation.

We have looked at *my* perspectives on how I work with certain individuals and groups. We have even noted thoughts on recovery. At this final juncture I must speak to the added dimension essential to recovery in *my* work with eating disorders. I work primarily as part of a treatment team where the collaborative aspect is unique in an outpatient setting. As a therapist working with an individual, I have ready access to the physician, nutritionist, family therapist, group therapist, and psychiatrist (when applicable), all of whom may be working with my patient. We have all become accustomed to making ourselves available to one another, having had this precedent set by the director, who medically monitors and assesses each patient. We work as a team. Our patients know this. It becomes increasingly important to them as their treatment progresses. We as practitioners are all aware of the splitting that can occur in the treatment process, as reflected in one practitioner being "all good" one week, and another "all bad"; these same roles can reverse the very next week. An open communication line between members of the treatment team is a mandatory part of our philosophy. Although we continue to evolve daily, this essential aspect of our treatment approach remains a solid and consistent base for all our efforts to promote recovery.

References

Bruch, Hilde. 1982. "Psychotherapy in Anorexia Nervosa." *International Journal of Eating Disorders* 1 (summer): 3–14. As cited in Dan W. Reiff and Kathleen Kim Lampson. 1992. *Eating Disorders: Nutrition Therapy in the Recovery Process*, 469. Aspen, Md.: Aspen Institute Publications.

Dickstein, Leah J. 1989. "Current College Environments: Do These Communities Facilitate and Foster Bulimia in Vulnerable Students?" In Leighton C. Whitaker and William N. Davis, eds., *The Bulimic College Student: Evaluation, Treatment, and Prevention*, 107–33. New York: Haworth.

Gordon, Richard A. 1989. "Bulimia: A Sociocultural Interpretation." In Leighton C. Whitaker and William N. Davis, eds., *The Bulimic College Student: Evaluation, Treatment, and Prevention*, 41–55. New York: Haworth.

Jones, D. M. 1985. "Bulimia: A False Self-Identity." *Clinical Social Work Journal* 13:305–16. As cited in Richard A. Gordon. 1989. "Bulimia: A Sociocultural Interpretation," in Leighton C. Whitaker and William N. Davis, eds., *The Bulimic College Student: Evaluation, Treatment, and Prevention*, 41–55. New York: Haworth.

Lonergan, Elaine Cooper. 1992. "Using Group Therapy to Foster the Psychosexual Development of Patients with Eating Disorders." *Group* 16 (summer): 85–94.

Wolf, Naomi. 1991. *The Beauty Myth: How Images of Beauty Are Used against Women*. New York: Morrow.

13

Recovery

MARGARET GOLDKOPF-WOODTKE

> For a long moment I stood before my own image, coming to knowl-
> edge of myself. Suddenly I saw all I was supposed to be but was not—
> taller, more ethereal, more refined, less hungry, not so powerful,
> much less emotional, more subdued, not such a big talker; a more
> generous, loving, considerate, nurturant person; less selfish, less
> ambitious, and far less given to seeking pleasure for myself.
>
> Now, however, all this came into question: Who, I wondered,
> had made up this ideal for women? Who had imposed it, and why
> hadn't I seen through it before? Why, for that matter, did I imagine
> a slender body would bring me these attainments, even if I decided
> I actually wanted them for myself? And why, finally, wasn't I free
> simply to throw off this whole coercive system of expectation and be
> myself—eating, lusting, laughing, talking, taking?
>
> —*The Obsession*, Kim Chernin

I was asked to write this paper from the position of both a professional and a recovered anorexic. I am frequently asked about recovery, both by my patients and those close to me, those who witnessed
the transformation that took place in my own life as a result of the
recovery process.

I had promised myself that were I truly to recover from anorexia
nervosa, I would someday communicate to others who also suffer
from eating disorders the "how" of recovery. I had imagined a step-
by-step approach that would somehow end the terrible obsession.

My goal in writing this paper is to integrate both my personal and professional experiences. I hope that by discussing my own recovery, as well as describing how that journey now aids me in my work with eating disordered patients, I will provide useful information to the practitioner and hope for patients and their families.

The pain of recovery is difficult to describe, the raw exposure that comes from peeling away layers of feelings. Because no step-by-step approach exists, knowing exactly where to begin is difficult.

I believe four basic ingredients are necessary to provide fertile ground for the recovery process to occur. Acceptance that a problem exists, combined with a desire to get well, inner strength, and hope, were central elements to me, and these same elements are often expressed by other recovered persons. All four may not be present at the start but do surface as recovery progresses.

Acceptance needs to occur at two different levels of understanding: (1) recognizing that one has a problem; and (2) admitting that one cannot deal with this problem alone. For someone with an eating disorder, arriving at these levels of understanding can be devastating. Frequently the eating disordered patient up to this point has offered the persona of the well-put-together individual. This is the persona she feels she must give to her world. Most people accept this perception as true and reinforce it—to be perfect and "problemless" is the only acceptable way to take up space in a world already burdened with so many ills.

I had set up so many expectations for myself and had tried desperately to give everyone what I believed they wanted or needed from me. How could I let them down by expressing how truly unhappy I was, how weak I felt, perhaps even how angry I was that I had to be this person? How could I accept that my way of "being," a way of life that had worked for so long, was not working anymore? This was, perhaps, the primary letting go in the process of recovery.

I should mention here the number of times I have heard patients say: "When I told my parents (doctor, coach, friend) that I thought I had a problem, that I might be anorexic or bulimic, they told me I was overreacting, that I'm too 'put together' for that. Once I relieved some of the stress in my life, I would feel better." Responses such as these only reinforce the fear of disappointing others.

When eating disordered patients first come to me for treatment,

I can appreciate both the difficulty and the pain they suffer as they try to express to me that they no longer can do it alone. Months may pass before a patient can let down her guard. Trusting the therapist does not come easily, especially if that trust has been violated in the past.

Patients often come to treatment because they have been forced or coaxed. They have not yet accepted the fact that they have an eating disorder. Their priority is to be thin, and they believe they are fat. Although this perception of themselves may be distorted, it is their perception. I understand its reality. I shared that perception myself.

I can tell you from personal experience that the attempt simply to erase that perception is neither helpful nor possible. That self-image, that distorted image, is clung to vigorously. To me those perceptions were everything; without them I was nothing. My body was my only way of expressing my dissatisfaction with my life. By not eating I felt a sense of power; by the feeling of hunger, a sense of control. When life felt "crazy" around me, when my parents fought, when my opinion differed from someone else's, when I felt angry and unable to express my anger, I starved myself and felt in control.

Because it is counterproductive to impose my own perception on a patient, I find it more beneficial to address the unhappiness the patient brings into treatment. Often the patient is unhappy for having to seek help. An eating disorder is a symptom of something going wrong in a person's life. Focusing in this direction often engages the patient and offers her an arena in which to explore her confusion, fears, and feelings.

Patience on the part of the therapist goes hand in hand with acceptance. Essentially the therapist also must accept how threatening it feels for a patient to open up.

A part of me wanted my therapist to jump in and save me, to push the treatment along, not just to listen to my sadness. I wanted her to tell me exactly what I needed to do to make everything better. In retrospect, had it happened that way, I never would have learned that the answers and the strengths were within me.

That desire to "jump in" and save my patients is a vulnerability I have to keep in check as I work with them. I often just want to take their pain away. I know how much I needed to feel in control of the process, a process that was frightening at times. My control over my own therapy is what ultimately empowered me to keep going, to learn about myself and my needs. It was as though my therapist and I joined forces to sift through the "stuff" in my life.

I admit one is tempted at times to take that power away from patients, especially when they present as helpless. Unfortunately this loss of power is often what they have experienced in their lives and within their families. To avoid reproducing this experience in therapy is difficult. Recognizing it when it does occur, however, is essential. Therapists, in their attempt to avoid overprotecting their patients, are often somewhat detached as a result. This is a delicate balance that must be achieved in the therapeutic alliance.

In my experience, feeling powerless created a feeling of helplessness, and underneath it all was a great deal of anger. Anger was a difficult emotion for me to identify, admit, or express. Anger in its most passionate form is rage, which is not considered an attractive trait in a woman. I was afraid of my anger, afraid of how potent it could be. Anger and eating were intimately tied. If I ate I was convinced I would be fat. If I let my anger out, I felt I might explode.

Therapy provided me the setting to explore this very real emotion of anger and this very real part of myself. A long time passed before I could talk about my angry feelings without defending the objects of my anger. I feared that if I expressed what I felt, I would alienate those I needed most, including my therapist. Exploring my anger was difficult but ultimately helped me feel safer and less helpless.

Hope is another essential ingredient to recovery. Exactly where the hope comes from is difficult to explain. For me, the feeling of hope changed and grew in intensity as I changed and grew. Initially it came from without, from the external changes in my life, along with my new working relationships with therapist, doctor, and nutritionist. Eventually it came from within, from all I learned to accept and appreciate within myself.

Some patients go from therapist to therapist or situation to situation searching for hope. I can remember clearly leaving an initial session with a new therapist, the one who ultimately journeyed with me, knowing I felt something different. This was after struggling three years with various therapists and medical doctors. Amid all the confusion and pain, I finally felt some hope. I did not know what it meant. I certainly could not imagine being free of a food and weight obsession or of being truly happy. I just sensed a possibility that something could change. I did not always feel so hopeful through-out my years of treatment, but I could always be reminded of it as I progressed.

If I examine what else was going on in my life at the time, I can see more clearly why I finally began to see light in what felt like total darkness. Many changes were occurring simultaneously, which were actually providing me with more control and more possibilities. I had made a life choice that was not healthy for me. It followed a long-standing pattern of pleasing others and an inability to look at my own needs. This theme is not uncommon for anorexics or bulim-ics. Once I decided to reexamine that choice, I uncovered a whole range of emotions and possibilities. This was extremely frightening, as it was a major risk for someone uncomfortable with the unknown. However, it was a step I needed to take in my desire to get well. I understand now that there was much more to me than the pain and confusion I had known for years, or I could never have taken such a major step.

Along with my individual therapy, I also began nutritional coun-seling, group therapy, and medical observation, which included the use of an antidepressant. All this provided a support system I had never allowed myself. Though I had been struggling for years, I had never fully accepted the fact that I could not handle the situation alone. I was still trying to keep from burdening others. Now I found myself at a different place, the threshold of recovery. I felt afraid, even of the possibility of getting well, but, for some undefined rea-son, the act of giving in gave me hope.

This hope grew as I learned about myself in therapy, in a rela-tionship with someone who gave me permission to be in this fright-ening and painful place, someone who was not afraid of my feelings, and, more important, was not overwhelmed by me. My therapist gently helped me to peel away the layers of unexpressed emotion and to experience myself and my body in a healthier and more appropriate way. The warmth I felt toward her allowed me to begin exploring what it meant to become a woman. When I sat with her, when I talked with her, when I looked at her, I was less afraid of that potential in myself.

A major part of recovery is learning to tolerate uncomfortable feelings and painful emotions. Somewhere along the developmental line, a person with an eating disorder learns or interprets that these emotions are not okay, that you are somehow defective if you feel or express them. To keep from feeling and to be in control at all times becomes a constant struggle. No wonder patients have difficulty identifying, let alone expressing, what they are feeling. My parents had difficulty seeing me unhappy. In their attempt to protect me from the pains of growing up, they gave me a message: "Don't feel bad." When I did, I felt paralyzed. Their intention was not to be malicious, but the message got muddled up for me. This often happens to eating disordered patients.

I know that patients need to feel that the therapist can tolerate their feelings and accept them. At the same time the therapist needs to be aware of her own reactions in order not to transmit similar messages. Speaking personally, I need to integrate my ability to identify and consequently to empathize with my patients, along with my ability to set limits or boundaries, respecting their needs. This balance, I believe, can provide the hope I have been speaking of.

One goes through stages of recovery, as well as areas or experiences, that need to be addressed and readdressed.

The physical self can no longer be avoided, as the mind and body are so intimately connected. The bottom line for most eating disordered patients is that they need to gain weight or accept the weight at which their body seems comfortable. Sometimes this is essential before true intrapsychic work can be done, and hospitalization may be deemed necessary. One cannot recover without beginning to let go of the symptoms—the starving, the bingeing, the excessive exercising, the purging.

For me, letting go of the symptoms and gaining weight was a process in itself. I can remember literally holding myself down at times so I would not go out and exercise. I also needed to force myself to drink a nutritional supplement to increase caloric intake. The discomfort was frequently intolerable. I often cried. I kept telling myself, "If I can just get through a month of this, then I'll know I won't have to get fat." I had to trust what my nutritionist had told me.

Tolerating this discomfort was the beginning of learning to tolerate other uncomfortable feelings, such as anger, anxiety, and dependence. Only after a long while did I not feel the urge to return to old patterns or means of control, and when I did, that too became uncomfortable. Nothing worked anymore. Running from my feelings became as uncomfortable as feeling them. Now I had choices, and this was progress. Progress, however, was frightening. I have often told people that at times my recovery was more difficult than being "sick." The desire to get well is an essential first step, but enduring the treatment can feel impossible at times. Getting better means one has to say good-bye to some very old friends—one's symptoms—and the loss needs to be grieved.

As a therapist, I find that seeking the aid and expertise of a nutritionist is helpful. Personally it was a must in my own recovery. This support correlates to the therapy as the patient is guided through the physical changes that occur and is encouraged to make these changes by someone other than therapist, doctor, or family. Simultaneously the work of learning to tolerate feelings is occurring in therapy.

In the same vein, the eating disordered patient needs to be evaluated and followed by a physician, primarily because of the medical risks. I spoke earlier of the mind/body connection; it follows that the medical, nutritional, and therapeutic means must be integrated. At first I felt that I just needed to feel better physically. I was so entrapped by my symptoms that I could not focus on anything else. This is true for many eating disordered patients. I was so in tune with my physiological self that my digestion and my bloated stomach were foremost on my mind. I believed that this is what made me unhappy. When I was forced to seek out a doctor, several tries were needed to find someone sensitive and aware of what I was experiencing. A part of me knew that I needed to gain weight, but another part needed to be in complete control. Two physicians told me to go home and eat; another said that my stomach problems were the result of stress and worry, so I should stop worrying. Not until I met a doctor who understood that much more underlay my symptoms was recovery made possible. I remember my first visit to that doctor, and asking, "How long will it take me to feel better?" I also remember the response, "Maybe by next summer you'll begin to feel better." I think I felt angry, certainly challenged, but I did not miss my next appointment. I did not hear what I wanted to hear, but it must have been what I needed to hear. I wanted a quick fix, but when the other doctors offered me that, I felt misunderstood and alone. Finally someone understood. She did not negate or ignore my symptoms. In fact, she focused on them and let me know they were real. She did not stop there. Once I felt listened to, I allowed her to hear my pain and she helped me look at my options. I had wanted my therapist to take away my sadness, as I now wanted my doctor to take away my symptoms.

My relationship with all three of these helping professionals was unique and powerful. Each was exposing, challenging, and support-ive. It was exposing to have to get on a scale. It was exposing to have to discuss what I ate. It was exposing to have to express what I felt. I say all this to reinforce the importance of integrating the mind and body. Symptoms get played out in all aspects of a patient's life. To separate these pieces seems futile.

Discussing one's symptoms in therapy, individual or group, is somewhat controversial. Patients have told me that a previous ther-apist did not allow or believe it useful to spend time or energy in this realm. Although going directly to the underlying issues can be valu-able, ignoring the symptoms and how a patient feels about those symptoms is missing a crucial part of the recovery process. An essen-tial aspect of therapy is respect for where the patient is. Some patients need to talk about their symptoms; others avoid it. No hard or fast rule exists except to flow with the patient.

As I discussed above, initially the obsession, the symptoms, and the behaviors feel like the source of the major discomfort. At times I would go into a session feeling anxious about my weight or I would be thinking only about my desire to eat something. I could not understand how all this connected to my family, my work, my rela-tionships, and so forth. All I felt at the time was desperation. This was the part of me I felt ashamed of, the part of me I hated. I needed to be able to talk about this. Perhaps it was avoidance, but talking about it led me to what I was avoiding. When I didn't talk about it, I felt deceptive, as though I were hiding from my therapist, as I hid from the rest of the world. If I could not talk about it at my therapy session, then where?

As time went on, I more fully understood and experienced the connection between my symptoms and my feelings, my way of coping. Even with that understanding, I often needed to return and talk about the behavior and the shame. I felt I had let so many people down, including myself.

Sometimes therapy intensified the obsession. Symptoms can get played out in therapy and can be useful to the therapist. This can signal that something is going on in the relationship.

Initially the more dependent I felt on my therapist, the more obsessive I became. Being able to talk about all this helped me to learn, as well as to experience, the connection between my inability to eat and my fear of growing and separating from those to whom I felt attached. This also aided in strengthening an alliance with my therapist, who did not treat me with disgust or bewilderment. Her acceptance helped to ease my shame and helped me to address it.

Therapists must be aware of their own feelings about the behaviors that an eating disordered patient brings to therapy. The therapist's own discomfort may cause the patient to resist talking about such primitive behaviors. One also needs to examine one's own feelings about weight, food, and body image, as these messages can get transmitted.

The patient needs to recognize that letting go of symptoms is part of, but different than, letting go of obsessing. Much more work needs to be done before one can give that up. I would often question whether I was truly getting better since the food and weight obsession, though lessened, still had a place in my life. I recognize now that the obsessing was the last to go. As I became fulfilled in other ways, through my personal and professional life, I no longer needed the obsession.

An outsider, a therapist, a family member, or a friend can easily get excited and hopeful on seeing symptoms decrease, such as when the patient gains weight or reports that purging has ceased. One needs to remember that this is only a part of recovery and that the sufferer may not be as excited or hopeful. A patient has difficulty hearing someone say, "You look good" or "You look healthy." This is often heard as "You look fat" and creates panic. Initially the feeling of being bigger, fuller, is awful. Others need to be sensitive to this.

A patient recently expressed a situation to me that brought back vivid memories. She reported trying on old clothes that were sizes too small, and consequently very tight. She told me she "freaked out"—cried and screamed for about half an hour, and then decided she needed to get rid of them all. This felt like a turning point. Those tight clothes reflected so many of her fears and gave her the opportunity to emote her anger at having to give up that control, at having to change. She had to look at her struggle with needing more food and taking up more space.

At times I just wanted to disappear. I felt I was not entitled to take up space because I was imperfect. Losing the weight was like losing myself. I was also sending out a signal that something was wrong. As ashamed as I was, I wanted someone else to see my pain and to help me with it. I wanted to be understood. I wanted to know that I was loved and accepted no matter what. It took a great deal of work—the work of recovery—to allow me to let go of the life-threatening mask I had learned to wear. It took growing, in every sense of the word. "As a child she is praised and rewarded with approval for being 'good' when she puts on a smiling and cheerful face. No attention is paid to the painful underlying misery, of which she too is scarcely aware" (Czyzewski and Suhr 1988).

Growing up is not an easy process, but the attempt to arrest that process is even more difficult. Going forward is often frightening and filled with fear and uncertainty; a person may attempt to stop or interrupt this movement forward.

Growing up means that the body must change and develop. It means separating, taking risks, and moving away from parents. Growing up means making decisions and making mistakes. It means growing into a more sexual being, feeling new sensations, and getting to know one's body in a more intimate way. Growing up is filled with mixed emotions and often mixed messages. It offers challenge, excitement, change, choices, as well as fear, disappointment, responsibilities, and the eventual enduring of many necessary losses. In a nutshell, growing up can be overwhelming and has much in common with recovery.

As I listen to patients talk about their experiences growing up, their concerns and beliefs, their fears about moving beyond their parents, and their discomfort with getting bigger, their struggles make a great deal of sense to me. The world we live in is not such a safe place, and our own personal worlds may feel even less so. Our culture places many expectations on women; although some of those expectations are changing, we are still caught in the middle, battling the transition.

Eventually I learned that recovery did not mean getting rid of the fears. Instead, it meant moving forward in spite of them. Essentially it meant giving up the need to control my world so tightly. I had to learn to tolerate uncertainty and not to be controlled by the pressures placed on myself as a woman to be thin, passive, and pleasing.

Listening to a patient takes on many different forms. "The most fundamental skill of the psychotherapist is productive listening. Everything else the therapist does needs to be founded on his developed ability to hear on many levels simultaneously. Such listening is much more than passive recording; it is a dynamic alertness which involves many sense modalities plus intuition, reflection, and cultivated empathy" (Bugenthal 1987).

What has become essential in my work as I listen to patients is my ability to also hear what is happening inside me. My own feelings often give me vital information about what my patient might be experiencing or avoiding. This countertransference challenges me to continue my own growth personally and professionally. If used appropriately, it can also challenge the patient.

For example, one patient may come in ready to talk about her discomfort with her body and her fear of gaining weight. She reports feeling out of control and then brings up her fear about moving into a new relationship. Sexually she feels inadequate, yet desirous. She reports having difficulty dealing with her need to please and her guilt about wanting to be pleased. I hear her plight; as we begin to explore her feelings, I find myself feeling angry that we live in a society where women are still confronted with these conflicts. I also feel sad, as I sense the pain that accompanies her fear. I wonder if she feels angry or sad, though at the moment she is only expressing self-disgust at her lack of discipline. "Maybe I am just not hard enough on myself." I do not want to impose my feelings on her; but, for the time being, I make a mental note of the messages I am getting.

Another example is when I feel stuck in a session or a number of sessions. This often means that the patient is feeling the same way.

What is keeping us stuck may be a subtle collusion on my part to avoid moving into some feelings that I, too, find uncomfortable.

This situation occurred recently as a patient was describing her relationship with her now-deceased mother. As she struggled to move through her guilt and shame in order to allow herself to feel angry at this woman who had been unable to meet her needs as a child, I too found myself struggling. I had to struggle to try not to protect her from these feelings, as I had wanted to be protected, nor to protect her mother, who may not have known better, much like I had wanted to protect my mother.

Protecting my family felt much safer than looking at what my body was telling me. It was a challenge to let myself feel angry and cheated, since I feared losing my parents' love and admiration. How could I be so disloyal to the two people who loved me the most? More important, how could I survive if I were to lose that love? Participating in a therapy group facilitated this process for me. Being in a supportive environment that at times felt like a family, I was able to express and test out what I was genuinely feeling.

I believe my parents did the best they could and never meant for me to suffer in any way. Unfortunately, at certain critical points in my development, this was not enough. Do I blame them? No. But I did need to explore the impact these crucial relationships had on me. I needed to give myself permission to deal with what was lacking, what was not so positive, before I could recognize the strengths that were given to me as well. That I was capable of building a positive alliance with my therapist was proof that I was already using one of my strengths, a way of relating to another, who at the time was very much like a parental figure. Though, as Hilde Bruch would point out, while many misconceptions about myself needed to be exposed and corrected, some very positive aspects of my personality also needed to be recognized and owned.

As a therapist, I sometimes have difficulty bringing a patient back to painful memories or experiences that may have fostered these misconceptions. I am not immune to these experiences, and although they do not have the same power in my life, they do hold a place. I recognize this even more since becoming a mother. Many issues that seemed to have been laid to rest through my own therapy begin to emerge again in a new way.

My pregnancies and mothering have had a significant impact on my work as a therapist. During my pregnancies, I once again had to experience my body growing and changing. Much of the time during the early months of pregnancy I had little or no control over how I felt physically. This brought back horrible memories and feelings at a time when I was supposed to be happy and full of life.

Once again, I experienced the disappointed looks from those who loved me and found it difficult to tolerate my feelings. I recognized how easily I had slipped back into taking so much care of everyone else. The difference this time, as a recovered person, was that I could call on the resources I had developed through therapy; I knew I needed to take care of me, whatever the cost. My response to the situation was a healthier one, though the conflict was just as painful.

I did not immediately inform my patients when I knew that I was pregnant, although some of them appeared to be keenly aware that something was different. I seemed less available, and some patients felt I had abandoned them. I felt guilty that my emotional energy was now turned inward and that others were getting less of me. Of course, this is true for all of us in this profession at different times in our lives. Again, it is a matter of learning how to use these significant times productively with patients.

Clinical supervision was essential for me during both my pregnancies as it helped me sort out my feelings. Initially I defended my position on a subtle level with patients. In doing so, I avoided the emergence of important material. Once I worked these feelings through, I was better able to help patients deal with their own feelings of abandonment in their lives.

Abandonment is a frightening and painful issue and resonates with many eating disordered patients. The fear of being left, especially if one is not perfect or deserving, is very real. I became even more empathic toward my patients' feelings about abandonment after the birth of my second child. At the time I was intimately involved with my first child's feelings of being pushed aside. I could also understand on a deeper level what I must have experienced as a child, being one of six children. How much I wanted to protect my firstborn from such painful feelings, yet I knew I could not. As I have mentioned before, the same holds true for my patients. Often I want to protect them in the same way. Instead, the best I can do is to support them consistently through the very human experiences that are part of any meaningful relationship.

I think it is important here to describe briefly the experience of being pregnant—of growing bigger, of watching my belly, my thighs, and my breasts expand. Although it may be hard for eating disordered patients to believe, it was a wonderful experience for me. As the uncomfortable physical symptoms subsided, I began to feel full of life, in every sense of the word. I enjoyed my round belly and full breasts, parts of my body I had spent years punishing myself for. I felt sensual, a feeling I had worked hard denying. My being exposed in such a sexual and feminine way created anxiety on the part of my patients. It also fostered openness. Some patients were able to begin talking about their own sexuality, their own desires and fears. I, too, was less afraid to venture into this intimate area of concern.

I believe my fond feelings toward my body as it continued to grow were evident. This in itself, I feel, was a gift to some of my patients, an opportunity to see that other ways exist of viewing and embracing one's body as a woman.

Becoming a parent has been yet another experience that has helped me grow and let go beyond my wildest imaginings. It has also pushed old buttons, as well as given me new vision professionally. Since I have become the mother of two enchanting daughters, my ability to empathize has grown stronger. As I watch them grow, I often wonder if my struggle to support them through their developmental stages would be different had they been sons. My response is, I hope not, yet I cannot help but wonder. Contradictions abound today. How do we teach our daughters to be assertive, strong, expressive, and confident, as well as nurturing, kind, respectful, and compassionate? How do we teach them that when striving not to be selfish, one does not have to be selfless?

Today we tell our children that it is okay to have feelings, that it is okay to be angry. But do we really give them the freedom to express that anger as they move through stages of growth and assertion that are filled with frustration and confusion? I believe many mixed messages are conveyed to young girls today.

I listen to patients' pain around growing and separating. I hear them say: "I used to be so good, so nice—everything seemed perfect. Now I hate myself and it's an effort just to smile."

They seem to be living proof of that very contradiction, and nothing anyone can say will make it easier. Now they work at defining themselves in a new way, feeling terrified of who they might become. I see their strong wills and gentle souls trying to merge—strengths that have become an illness because the conflict is too much to bear.

I see beautiful women, young and old, loathing their bodies because they do not quite meet society's standards for thin and firm.

I wonder how I will protect my daughters from all this. How do I help them embrace who they are and know they have something wonderful to contribute because they are both strong and sensitive—in essence, how do I protect them from all that I struggled with as a young woman and continue to confront as a mature woman in today's society?

Having daughters has made me recall some of my own struggle at different stages in my life. In turn, it has helped me to be more sensitive to my patients.

I have come to understand more fully the pain of a parent who has to learn, as I do, that we cannot protect our children from everything. Knowing when to protect or support or guide or let go is a complex part of parenting, as our own desires to have had these needs met in our own childhood may surface.

A bit should be added here about the family's struggle. Initially, eating disorders may get translated in families as just a problem involving weight loss and food. Parents feel helpless, frustrated, responsible, and often angry at the control being exercised by the child because of her illness and symptoms. They need to be helped and often educated about anorexia and bulimia.

Patients often report feeling guilty about how their eating disorder is affecting their family. At the same time they are crying out for help—for themselves and for their family. In therapy they may talk about the pressure they feel to be the model child or their desire to make everyone happy. They want to be separate yet fear the thought of it. They have a difficult time owning their right to life and enjoyment, despite their parents' plight.

I thought that getting the perspective of a mother who experienced recovery through her daughter might be helpful. I asked my own mother for her insight. She expressed the helplessness I spoke of and the fear that I would never be well again. She told me: "It was a nightmare. You just looked so forlorn, so unhappy. All I wanted to do was hold you and tell you it would be okay. That upset you even more, because you knew I could not possibly understand the complexity of your illness, what you were going through. Your illness consumed me. The frustration was that I had no idea how to help you, so I had to get help for myself."

She also expressed feeling responsible and guilty. She recalled: "I had to struggle with the guilt I felt all the time, knowing that even though it had not been on purpose, somehow I was related to the cause of this dreadful illness. I did not know what I had done wrong, but I suffered the fact that I was involved by something I had or had not done, however inadvertently."

Families can also recover and be helped through this process. To quote my mother again, "As I look back now I realize that this was a journey you needed to take—I felt that the day you could laugh at yourself and your imperfections was a great step, and something to celebrate."

Every patient's story is unique. It is possible that relationships with family members cannot be healed in the same way that mine could. This, however, does not mean that healing within the individual is not possible.

I have given a few examples of countertransference, whereby what I began feeling in a session gave me information about my patient and about myself. I would like to add that what I find myself taking on or experiencing with a patient can also give me essential clues about how a person interacts with others, what kind of feelings she may evoke in them.

Relating to a resistant teenager who was in treatment with me, I found myself feeling angry and helpless at times. When I was able to engage the family in treatment, it was telling to see these same feelings being enacted by the parents and siblings. Along with that, I needed to recognize my own feelings of helplessness when I have no control over a situation, some of my own memories of being a teenager, and my patient's desperate need to be in control. I needed to understand my own reactions more clearly so I could better understand my patient, and thus respond more appropriately, and perhaps differently, than the rest of her world.

Self-disclosure remains a highly controversial issue. This fact needs to be mentioned at this point, as the very process of writing this paper has made me expose myself in a very personal way. I have also spoken to groups about recovery and, in doing so, have disclosed a part of myself to patients. This adds another dynamic to the therapeutic experience.

Alan Ivey (1983) talks about self-disclosure as a skill, one that is utilized whenever a therapist uses an "I" statement or expresses a personal thought or feeling: "It is a form of self talk, and the complex task is in making this self talk relevant to the client."

Some patients seek me out because they know my history. My presence alone creates a sense of hope for them. This, however, can turn into competition, even hostility, especially when therapy becomes more difficult. It is important for me not to avoid these feelings. Avoidance on both our parts would certainly hinder our relationship and our ability to work productively together.

Some patients who have this so-called advantage of knowing my history (and even some who do not) will ask indirect questions or make general comments, as if searching for something. It is as though their connection to me will somehow magically make things better. I often have to work harder with patients who know about my recovery, to maintain appropriate boundaries and not attempt to fix their problems quickly.

I also find that self-disclosure has advantages. Patients have expressed having less difficulty with openness earlier in treatment. They expect that because I have been "there," I will understand and make sense out of it for them. I tell them, "Yes, I understand, but I cannot make sense out of it without you. That is our job together."

When I speak to interest groups and support groups, my goal is to provide hope and helpful information, as well as to be a positive role model. I find that this can transfer to therapy.

Some patients express both relief and frustration that they cannot hide from me, especially in terms of symptoms or defense mechanisms. I do not think this is entirely true, but it certainly adds more grist for the therapeutic mill.

Throughout this paper I have been discussing basic understandings as well as underlying themes that seem to resonate within individuals suffering with, and recovering from, anorexia and bulimia.

However, many stereotypes and generalizations clearly get over-played and overused. They can also be offensive. I am always angered to hear a colleague make derogatory statements about an eating disordered patient or to read material that does the same; for example, the statement "I hate working with these patients; they are so manipulative and deceptive" or "All eating disordered patients are borderline."

On one level I admit that it hurts and saddens me that this disorder is so misunderstood. Perhaps the basic drives and fears that must be addressed in therapy provoke too many uncomfortable feelings. Perhaps the patient's feelings of worthlessness are too much for the therapist to bear. Whatever the reasoning, I believe we should be more cautious when responding to one another, checking our own reactions before speaking or acting them out. We owe this respect to our patients and to one another.

I began this paper by stating that I am often asked about recovery. More specifically, I am asked how I knew I had recovered. One of my hopes in writing this paper is that the reader will come to understand the complexity of that question.

Had I recovered once I gained back enough weight to have my menstrual cycle return? Had I recovered once I could tolerate wear-ing bigger sizes? Had I recovered when I happened to glance at my chart in the doctor's office, which read, "Diagnosis—Anorexia Ner-vosa/Recovered"? Had I recovered when I could express anger appropriately? Had I recovered when I could start making impor-tant life decisions based on my needs? Had I recovered when I could listen to my hunger? Had I recovered when I could tolerate uncom-fortable feelings without starving myself? Had I recovered when I could laugh again?

The best answer I can offer to all these questions is that all these experiences were a part of my recovery, and not necessarily in the order I wrote them. They happened. Through therapy, through commitment to my own well-being, and through support, recovery happened! By dealing with my pain, facing my fears, it became pos-sible for me to grow—in every way.

I also need to say that full recovery is possible. Patients need to stay committed to their work even after symptoms disappear. The journey is long but one that does have a light at the end of the tunnel. All that I feared, the hurts I felt, even the desire to be on top of things, have not disappeared. I am, fortunately, still a human being but one who is living life more fully, thankful for the privilege of being a part of other patients' journeys, and especially thankful for the great gifts of faith, hope, and laughter!

References

Bugenthal, James F. 1987. *The Art of the Psychotherapist*. New York: Norton.

Chernin, Kim. 1981. *The Obsession: Reflections on the Tyranny of Slenderness*. New York: Basic Books.

Czyzewski, Darita, and Melanie A. Suhr. 1988. *Hilde Bruch: Conversations with Anorexics*. New York: Basic Books.

Ivey, Allen. 1983. *Intentional Interviewing and Counseling*. Monterey, Calif.: Brooks/Cole.

Afterword

DIANE W. MICKLEY

I really never thought I'd get out of that stupid anorexia-bulimia
cycle, but I did. Please let people who are having problems know
that there is a way out.

—Outcome Study, The Wilkins Center, 1987

In the previous papers, clinicians have shared glimpses of their experiences treating eating disordered patients and their families. Ideally
we could draw from the practice and literature of the last decade and
conclude with clear guidelines for treatment. In 1993 the American
Psychiatric Association published a set of official recommendations
for the treatment of eating disorders; recently an updated revision
has been issued (Work Group on Eating Disorders 2000). Yet crucial questions remain unresolved. Who can expect a favorable outcome? Which treatment approach is suitable for each patient? How
intensive should treatment be, and how long should it last? How can
we lessen the likelihood of relapse?

Surprisingly few factors correlate consistently with outcome
(Herzog et al. 1991; Sohlberg, Norring, and Rosmark 1992). Clinically we see teenagers with mild and recent symptoms who struggle
to improve. We also see women with decades of bulimia who respond

surprisingly rapidly to treatment. Some patients flounder despite enormously supportive families; others succeed despite families that are geographically or emotionally unable to be involved. Patients with seemingly mild symptoms may have persistent difficulties; others may be extremely symptomatic and yet make impressive and complete recoveries.

In 1987 we surveyed the first three hundred patients with anorexia or bulimia or both who had contacted the Wilkins Center (Mickley 1988). Many had been treated by our staff; others had been referred to hospitals, had moved to other geographic locations, or had chosen other treatment or none at all. All were two to five years from their first visit, and almost half had completed an evaluation.

Fifty percent of surveyed patients were considered to have recovered, using stringent criteria (within 10 percent of normal weight, regular menstrual periods, and no binges or purges in more than six months). Some, however, still experienced excess concern with weight. Another 15 percent were of normal weight but purged occasionally (less than once a week). Combining these groups, at two to five years, more than two-thirds of patients were relatively free of eating disorder symptoms. Another 20 percent of patients still purged more than once a week, but significantly less than before treatment. Less than 15 percent of patients were no better than when first seen.

In analyzing this outcome study, demographic data, including age, alcoholism in the patient or family, history of hospitalization, and duration of illness, had no statistical bearing on outcome. Only two factors were significant. Patients who did well were more likely to sign their evaluation questionnaires, whereas those who did poorly more often submitted them anonymously. More important, *more than 60 percent of patients with the best outcomes had had at least two years of individual psychotherapy*. In contrast, more than 50 percent of those who failed to improve had participated in consistent treatment for less than three months.

Though a majority of patients in our 1987 survey recovered, current outcome may be even more favorable. Many patients in the study were still in treatment when contacted and continuing to improve. In addition, treatment in the nineties includes an array of options that were not available in the early eighties. Antidepressants, now widely used and of proven benefit in the treatment of eating disorders (Walsh 1991), were only beginning to be recognized as helping bulimia when these early patients were treated. The study ended before fluoxetine (Prozac) was even marketed in the United States. Although fluoxetine alone has been of enormous value and has been approved by the Food and Drug Administration specifically for the treatment of bulimia, an array of new medications of potential benefit has become available and these are widely used. Progress has been made in other treatment techniques and combinations as well. It is hoped that these strides will promote recovery in an ever greater majority of those with anorexia and bulimia.

More recent data actually confirm and expand the findings of our 1987 study. In terms of prognosis, other studies also note that few factors consistently predict outcome (Herzog et al. 1991; Sohlberg, Norring, and Rosmark 1992). However, earlier age at onset tends to improve prognosis in both anorexia and bulimia. Healthy parental relationships may correlate with better outcome in anorexia, whereas good friendships may be associated with more favorable results in bulimia (Herzog, Nussbaum, and Marmor 1996).

Much subsequent research has analyzed outcome. Both anorexia and bulimia can be fatal illnesses, from either medical complications or suicide. Mortality in anorexia accrues at a rate of about 0.5 percent for each year of illness; that is, 5 percent of patients die after a decade of anorexia and 10 percent after two decades. The death rate in bulimia is less clear but probably lower. A 1997 review of eighty-eight outcome studies found that five to ten years after presentation, 50 percent of patients with bulimia had recovered from their eating disorder (although 30 percent had relapsed during the course of their illness), and up to 20 percent had chronic symptoms (Keel and Mitchell 1997). Some of the psychiatric difficulties seen during the acute illness may be secondary to the eating disorder and remit (Dancyger et al. 1997). However, even with complete eating disorder recovery, patients may experience other psychological difficulties, such as depression or anxiety disorders. Many studies have documented the need for intensive and long-term treatment, especially for anorexia (Herzog, Nussbaum, and Marmor 1996; Foppiani et al. 1998). It is impressive that the benefits of intensive psychological treatment can still be demonstrated five years after its completion (Eisler et al. 1997).

With eating disorders escalating around the globe, patients, as stated earlier, have come from Europe, Asia, and Latin America for treatment at the Wilkins Center. As with our American patients, treatment is most effective when tailored to these patients' particular family and cultural background. Emerging data support the benefits of adapting treatments to particular subsets of patients. Younger teens, for example, may benefit more from family therapy and a focus on maturity fears, whereas older patients may derive greater benefit from individual therapy and medication for depression and anxiety (Heebink, Sunday, and Halmi 1995; Eisler et al. 1997). Studies continue to demonstrate the high prevalence of borderline personality disorder among eating disordered patients (Wonderlich, Peterson, and Mitchell 1997). These individuals tend to have greater psychiatric difficulties and often require more extensive and enduring treatment.

The past twenty years have seen a burgeoning of new information in the field of eating disorders. Current studies are delineating the neurobiology of these illnesses and the genetic vulnerabilities to their development. Pharmacological and psychological treatments continue to expand and improve. Meanwhile, the advocacy movement continues to work for legislation and insurance coverage for patients who need intensive or long-term treatment. Finally, prevention efforts continue to address the cultural milieu that fosters eating disorders and the identification of young women with high risk of illness and those not receiving adequate treatment.

Strides in related fields also benefit patients with eating disorders. The expanding array of safer and more effective psychiatric medication has been helpful to many patients with eating disorders. New treatments for obesity have benefited some overweight patients with binge eating disorder. The most recent groups added at the Wilkins Center provide dialectical behavioral therapy (DBT) for a subset of suitable patients. DBT, developed by Marsha Linehan, Ph.D., professor of psychology at the University of Washington in Seattle, is a treatment for patients with borderline personality disorder and has been adapted to other settings. It helps patients develop techniques to regulate moods, reduce self-harming behaviors, and increase interpersonal effectiveness, skills very useful for a subgroup of patients with eating disorders.

Although total recovery is the ideal outcome, treatment may improve both the physical and emotional well-being of those whose recovery may not be complete. Though improved weight and cessation of purging are concrete signs of improvement, treatment should also promote better relationships, self-esteem, mood, and overall well-being. Helping the parents, siblings, partners, and children of those with eating disorders can also be of significant, if unmeasured, benefit.

Eating disorders can have a devastating effect on the lives of those affected. Treatment can be long and difficult, taxing the resources of patients and families, as well as the patience and skills of the treatment team. What justifies this enormous commitment if outcome is uncertain? Patients in our survey were offered the opportunity to volunteer any further observations they wished. A sample of their comments expresses the gratification of improvement and the triumph of recovery:

> I want you to know I really am all better. This year I've been dealing with some very drastic circumstances. My feelings are similar to the ones I felt in 1983 when I was bulimic. However, this time I didn't eat away my problems. I got back into therapy as quickly as I could.

> Both individual and group therapy helped me immeasurably. I learned to like myself and deal with issues that bothered me by talking about them—not eating my way around them.

> Dietary counseling was crucial. I feel that this, more than anything else, helped me to stop my bulimic and anorexic behavior so that I could deal with the emotional problems underlying the eating disorder.

> A different reality—

> I always basically knew food was not as much the problem as it was a lack of love, feeling alone, hating myself.

> I have a good understanding of what caused the disorder, but, more important, I have a much better sense of self-worth.

Treatment helped me to face life, its problems and its joys. I am much happier.

I am much better but much worse, because I am feeling now.

A connectedness—

It has been a long slow process involving changing years of destructive and maladaptive behavioral patterns.

If it weren't for [treatment], I would still be in the same rut. Thanks to you, I consider myself a "recovered bulimic." I am a relatively happy person—married and expecting my first child! Who would have thought I would be in this lucky position four years ago.

How deeply indebted I feel [for my treatment]. I was able to get pregnant (gained 40 pounds), and I have a wonderful healthy son. . . . Thank you for giving me back a relatively normal life.

And in summation, an ode to life—

Because of our work together, I am alive, well, and free.

References

Dancyger, I. F., S. R. Sunday, E. D. Eckert, and K. A. Halmi. 1997. "A Comparative Analysis of Minnesota Multiphasic Personality Inventory Profiles of Anorexia Nervosa at Hospital Admission, Discharge, and 10-Year Follow-up." *Comprehensive Psychiatry* 38 (3):185–91.

Eisler, I., C. Dare, G.F.M. Russell, G. Szmukler, D. le Grange, and E. Dodge. 1997. "Family and Individual Therapy in Anorexia Nervosa." *Archives of General Psychiatry* 54:1025–30.

Foppiani, L., L. Luise, E. Rasore, U. Menichini, and M. Gusti. 1998. "Frequency of Recovery from Anorexia Nervosa in a Cohort of Patients Reevaluated on a Long-term Basis Following Intensive Care." *Eating and Weight Disorders* 3:90–94.

Heebink, D. M., S. R. Sunday, and K. A. Halmi. 1995. "Anorexia Nervosa and Bulimia Nervosa in Adolescence: Effects of Age and Menstrual

Status on Psychological Variables." *Journal of the American Academy of Child and Adolescent Psychiatry* 35 (3): 378–82.

Herzog, D. B., M. B. Keller, P. W. Lavori, and N. R. Sacks. 1991. "The Course and Outcome of Bulimia Nervosa." *Journal of Clinical Psychiatry* 52 (10): 4–8. Supplement.

Herzog, D. B., K. M. Nussbaum, and A. K. Marmor. 1996. "Comorbidity and Outcome in Eating Disorders." *Psychiatric Clinics of North America* 19 (4): 843–59.

Keel, P. K., and J. E. Mitchell. 1997. "Outcome in Bulimia Nervosa." *American Journal of Psychiatry* 154:313–21.

Mickley, D. W. 1988. "Outcome of 300 Eating Disordered Patients Treated Between 1982 and 1985." Presented at the Scientific Sessions of the Third International Conference on Eating Disorders. New York.

Sohlberg, S. S., C.E.A. Norring, and B. E. Rosmark. 1992. "Prediction of the Course of Anorexia Nervosa/Bulimia Nervosa over Three Years." *International Journal of Eating Disorders* 12 (2): 121–31.

Walsh, B. Timothy. 1991. "Fluoxetine Treatment of Bulimia Nervosa." Journal of Psychodynamic Research 35 (1991): 33–40.

Wonderlich, S., C. Peterson, and J. E. Mitchell. 1997. "Body Image, Psychiatric Comorbidity, and Psychobiological Factors in Eating Disorders." *Current Opinion in Psychiatry* 10:141–46.

Work Group on Eating Disorders of the American Psychiatric Association. 1993. "Practice Guidelines for Eating Disorders." *American Journal of Psychiatry* 150 (2): 207–28.

———. 2000. "Practice Guidelines for Eating Disorders." *American Journal of Psychiatry* 157 (1). Supplement.

INDEX